What Your Colleagues Are Saying . . .

Margo Gottlieb and Andrea Honigsfeld's book, *Collaborative Assessment for Multilingual Learners and Teachers: Pathways to Partnerships,* is a timely and valuable resource. It tackles two crucial issues for K–12 language specialists:

- Fostering seamless collaboration between content and language teachers to facilitate effective content-based language learning
- Elevating the role of assessment to provide actionable data for immediate, short-term and long-term instructional decisions

This powerful duo cleverly links assessment with collaborative practices for a more equitable and assets-based approach. The creative artistic signals used along the way will help the reader tread and ponder over critical points of the framework. That will help facilitate reflection and implementation. A wonderful book on multilingual learner assessment!

—Dr. Margarita Calderón, Professor Emerita, Johns Hopkins University, MD

Embarking on the journey of collaborative assessment, readers of this book are the heroes being guided by the authors. A journey into collaborative instructional assessment cycles supports educators in learning to navigate the unfamiliar territory of interconnectedness and interdependence among multilingual learners, teachers, and families. Margo Gottlieb and Andrea Honigsfeld inspire educators to launch a transformative quest. Along the way, they introduce readers to friends traveling the same journey, supporting educators through obstacles and options. Reaching the destination, teachers have had experiences with integrating language and content, balancing instruction and assessment, and collaborating in implementing student-centered approaches. What a ride!

—Tamara J. Coburn, Lead ESL Teacher, Winston-Salem/Forsyth County Schools, NC

Using "journey" as a metaphor, Margo Gottlieb and Andrea Honigsfeld pool their extensive knowledge and experience to both zero in on and expand the day-to-day rhythms of collaborative assessment for multilingual learners. These urgently needed assessment practices, collected into their book and illustrated via vignettes, engender curiosity, collaborative conversations, and enquiring attitudes in teachers, students, and their families. This contrasts with the overreliance on one-and-done, high-stakes tests for accountability that often deflate and discourage, placing us all—especially multilingual students—into a deficit-oriented mindset rather than into a joyful journey of learning and growing together.

—Debra Cole, PhD, Postdoctoral Fellow, University of Missouri, St. Louis, MO

Bringing together Margo Gottlieb's equitable assessment practices and Andrea Honigsfeld's effective collaborative strategies, this book takes the reader on a stimulating learning journey to develop a practice of collaborative assessment. This valuable text is a must read for educators in schools implementing collaborative teaching models. It is also an excellent book for those interested in exploring new pathways toward multilingual learners' academic success. To transform your practice, get an extra copy for your partner.

—**Dr. Lori M. Edmonds, Assistant Professor of ESL Education,**
University of Alabama at Birmingham, AL

How can collaborative teaching for multilingual learners happen without collaborative planning? It cannot. And how can collaborative planning and teaching happen without authentic, embedded, and equally collaborative assessment? It should not. Margo Gottlieb and Andrea Honigsfeld definitely fill a logistical gap with this book, providing accessible, practitioner-friendly ideas for ways in which educators of multilingual learners can—and do—collaborate with their colleagues and their students to make assessment what it can be and should be. This book's journey toward collaborative assessment is one that positions planning, teaching, and assessing all as parts of the same collaborative endeavor, one that is done for and with multilingual students rather than to them. But it also asks all educators to truly see and value multilingual students for who they are and what they bring as assets to schools and communities everywhere.

—**Miriam Ehtesham-Cating, Director of Programs for Multilingual Learners,**
Burlington School District, Burlington, VT

This is an exciting book! I can't wait to share it with both EL and classroom teachers. It supports our work in professional learning communities and will help us continue to build strong coteaching relationships.

—**Tamara Eklöf-Parks, Multilingual Program Coordinator,**
Essex Westford School District, VT

We are all the most effective and creative when we collaborate with others. In Margo Gottlieb and Andrea Honigsfeld's new book, they demonstrate how collaboration and assessment go hand in hand to empower multilingual learners on a path to success. This practical addition to the field takes us on a journey that centers the readers' experience, providing evidence-based strategies and adaptable templates that promote collaborative assessment. Readers from all roles and levels of experience will easily engage with and apply this learning to their contexts. I highly recommend this book!

—**Dr. Diane Staehr Fenner, President, SupportEd and Author, VA**

In centering culturally and linguistically relevant and sustaining practices, multilingualism, learner variability, family engagement, and collaboration as normal, this book fills a gap in the assessment literature for multilingual students. Classroom teachers, ELD or bilingual teachers, and instructional coaches will find this resource highly useful as they work within communities of practice to plan collaborative classroom assessments that focus on multilingual student voice and choice to embed within the instructional and assessment cycle. This book is unique in the way it is creatively organized to take readers on a journey as they develop collaborative assessment practices. Important on this journey is an acknowledgment of the messy and sometimes challenging nature of the work and the authors' timely suggestions for how to work around potential obstacles as well as concrete strategies readers can modify or customize for their own local contexts. Various 'pit stops' sprinkled along the way allow readers to pause and reflect on how the text relates to their own assessment practices and context. I can't wait to use this text with my pre-service and mentor teachers!

—**Dr. Caitlin G. Fine, Assistant Professor, Metropolitan State University of Denver, CO**

"I no longer feel that I need to know and do it all . . . that's what colleagues are for . . . to share the responsibility for teaching our multilingual learners." This quote, from a seasoned educator, is at the heart of Margo Gottlieb and Andrea Honigsfeld's new book. When it comes to student assessment, teacher candidates are taught to rely on standards and standardized testing, often at the cost of their own intuitive understanding of students and issues of equity, social justice, and cultural diversity—specifically multilingualism. Teachers need a new road map. The design of this book as a collaborative journey—complete with road signs, roadblocks, and yes, even pit stops—is not only engaging but mirrors teaching and learning as an interactive and ongoing process. The belief that throughout this journey we must have multiple opportunities to meet up with and collaborate with our colleagues makes me eager to go on this journey along with my students.

—**Dr. Alice Ginsberg, Associate Director of Research, Rutgers University, NJ**

Margo Gottlieb and Andrea Hongisfeld have delivered again! In a time when many schools are unsure of assessment practices for multilingual learners, this book empowers educators to collaborate, share expertise, and cocreate assessment policies that truly serve all students. It is an essential resource for educators committed to creating equitable educational experiences and championing the strengths of diverse student populations.

—**Rob Greenhaw, Missouri Migrant and English Language Learning** (MELL)
Instructional Consultant, EducationPlus, St. Louis, MO

Margo Gottlieb and Andrea Honigsfeld build upon assets-based approaches, family engagement, and student voice; these values are close to my heart as an educator, therefore I immediately felt invested in this book. The vignettes make it easier to understand how the collaborative assessment ideas in this book could be implemented in my own building. Finally, this book is fun!!! I love how it is written like a journey that is meant to be engaged with. This text will make an excellent book study for coteaching teams or any team that wants to grow their collaborative assessment practices.

—Berth Harju, **Multilingual Learner Coteacher, Boise School District, ID**

Wow! I love this book so much; it is so needed. Many of the school districts that I work with have seen an increase in their multilingual learners and are eager to know how to best understand, assess, instruct, and support these students. This book provides all of that and more! It walks you through the collaborative process, shares incredible vignettes from classrooms and actual teachers, and provides you with powerful tools for better assessing, understanding, and supporting all your multilingual learners. Thank you Margo Gottlieb and Andrea Honigsfeld for creating this outstanding book and tool for all of us.

—Tami Hicks, **Director of WVEC Title III Consortium and Multilingual Learning,**
Wabash Valley Education Center, IN

As we strive toward a new and necessary season of education where multilingualism is the treasured norm, this book will guide our collective passion to collaboratively and effectively serve our brilliant students and families who have been historically marginalized by ineffective assessment systems. Beginning in early childhood and lasting through high school graduation, we can and must do better, together, and this resource will enlighten the journey.

—Kari Keith, **Director of Multilingual Programs,**
Community Consolidated School District 15, IL

Educators who need a comprehensive and practical resource on collaborative assessment will find this book to be invaluable, especially for their multilingual learners. Drawing from classroom examples, scholarship, and evidence-based teaching, Margo Gottlieb and Andrea Honigsfeld guide readers on a "journey" through collaborative assessment, illuminating key issues, challenges, and opportunities. This book is a must-read for teachers and other educators who are committed to supporting multilingual learners in K–12 settings.

—Ilka Kostka, PhD, **Teaching Professor, Northeastern University, MA**

Drs. Gottlieb and Honigsfeld, Margo and Andrea, brilliantly crafted this book to guide educators regarding collaborative assessment practices—with student agency at the center. Now, more than ever, our field must move beyond the widespread, inequitable decisions made based on high-stakes test data that, by design, repeatedly fall short in capturing MLs' true capabilities. Margo and Andrea offer real-world pathways to adopt collaborative, evidence-based assessment practices that showcase the countless dimensions of linguistic and cultural splendor MLs bring to our schools and communities.

—Dr. Joan Lachance, **Associate Professor, UNC Charlotte, NC**

Setting up an equitable playing field isn't always easy for teachers, so Drs. Margo Gottlieb and Andrea Honigsfeld provide clear and explicit answers to issues related to best practices in assessing multilingual learners. As we put adaptable classroom-ready templates and tools into practice, we can rest easy knowing that we are not only effectively addressing the assessment needs of our students, but we are also nurturing their overall academic and social-emotional needs. Their work is systemic, flexible, and inspirational because it provides multiple pathways for a collaborative assessment journey.

—Katie Leven, **NYS Itinerant ENL Teacher and Podcaster,**
The Intentional TESOL Podcast, NY

This book offers practical and thoughtful resources to guide pre- and in-service K–12 teachers in planning and implementing collaborative assessments as, for, and of learning. Given the strong emphasis on assessment in the current educational climate and how daunting assessment can feel for teachers, this is a much needed resource advocating for a culturally sustaining approach to the assessment of multilingual learners!

—Dr. Kathleen McGovern, **Assistant Professor of TESOL,**
The University of Southern Maine, ME

Margo Gottlieb and Andrea Honigsfeld have written a must-read K–12 practical guide for those of us who want to support multilingual learners' academic, linguistic, cultural, and social-emotional development through asset-based collaborative instruction and assessment. Read this book and join the extraordinary learning full of evidence-based strategies, ready-to-use tips, adaptable templates, and authentic examples. I can't wait to recommend this book to educators of multilingual learners in my network.

—Dr. Minh Hue Nguyen, **Senior Lecturer in TESOL/EAL, School of Curriculum,**
Teaching and Inclusive Education, Faculty of Education, Monash University, Australia

This book provides a framework for collaborative, equitable, and culturally and linguistically responsive assessment practices, helping educators to empower multilingual learners and create pathways for their success. Grounded in research-informed ideas that highlight the power of collaboration, this practical guide gives educators a road map for supporting schoolwide changes in assessing multilingual learners. Margo Gottlieb and Andrea Honigsfeld offer a wonderful example of the power of leveraging two areas of expertise (collaboration and assessment, respectively) in their first coauthored book. This practical guide can serve as an entry point for educators who seek to enhance assessment practices for content learning, language development, and literacy skills within an instructional cycle through collaboration. Never has there been such a need for collaborative works such as this one; *Collaborative Assessment for Multilingual Learners and Teachers: Pathways to Partnerships* will help educators of multilingual learners apply evidence-based strategies to their teaching practice and as a result, promote and support equitable assessment practices for this ever-growing population of students.

—Dr. Gretchen Oliver, **Assistant Professor & Co-Director of TESOL Programs,**
Siena College, NY

This book looks GREAT! It is really needed in the field. I get so many questions from teachers of bilingual students about appropriate assessments, and this book lays it out clearly in an approachable, well-written volume. So much of the discourse around assessment focuses on (English-centered) accountability and reflects a monolingual perspective—narrowly judging multilingual students' capacities by only counting what they can demonstrate in English in a summative test. This volume centers around honoring multilingual learners' unique skills and identities and helping educators learn how to work together to give students access to their full linguistic repertoire to demonstrate what they know and can do throughout their learning experiences.

—Deb Palmer, PhD (She/Ella), **Professor of Equity and Bilingualism/Biliteracy,**
University of Colorado Boulder, CO

Margo Gottlieb and Andrea Honigsfeld are the perfect combination when it comes to collaborative assessment for multilingual learners. In a linguistically and culturally diverse district, with over 100 languages spoken, this book will be invaluable to ensure we are taking strategic steps to assess our students with an asset-based approach. Honigsfeld's extensive study of collaborative practices for multilingual learners combined with Gottlieb's years of work with assessment and evaluation merge beautifully in the creation of meaningful and actionable ways to collaboratively assess student learning. Throughout the book, vignettes at the elementary, middle, and high school levels offer context for the content of their research. This book draws from the most current literature and provides multiple practical examples to guide us in making collaborative assessment practices a reality for our multilingual learners.

—Rita Pohlad, **Multilingual Learner (ML) Instructional Coach,**
Kentwood Public Schools, MI

As our district of over 1,000 multilingual learners invests in a strengthened, inclusive EL program model focusing on coteaching and integrated ELD, equitable assessment practices for multilingual learners has become a priority topic. This timely, relevant, and easy-to-read text is a must-read for educators at all levels who aim to enhance their assessment practices through an assets-based approach! From practical tips to adaptable templates, educators will be equipped with powerful tools to use right away. The authors weave vignettes from various educators around the United States and beyond throughout the text bringing the research and theory to life. We have seen the incredible impact of collaborative practices in various instructional settings, and we are anxious to roll up our sleeves to strengthen our collaborative assessment practices based on the combined expertise of Margo Gottlieb and Andrea Honigsfeld.

—Pamela Schwallier, PhD, **Director of EL and Bilingual Programs,**
West Ottawa Public Schools, MI

At NYS TESOL we believe all educators are educators of ELLs/multilingual learners. This book is an ideal tool for all teachers and administrators in many ways. High-quality systems, inclusive school culture, and the gradual release of responsibility are motifs throughout its pages. Furthermore, the asset-based ethos throughout this book can undoubtedly enhance school collaboration. As an educational leader and an ENL coteacher, it is clear to me that this book will help to build new and improved veteran relationships between coteachers and other educators. I say 'Yes!' this book is everything I'd like to communicate to colleagues. It is put so eloquently and succinctly via a metaphorical journey with vignettes of various school collaborative experiences. Thank you, Margo Gottlieb and Andrea Honigsfeld for putting this out for our schools . . . and truly, our society at large.

—Christine E. Seebach EdD, NYS TESOL, TESOL International, NYSCEA, NY

Collaborative Assessment for Multilingual Learners and Teachers is a must-have treasure for those who take on challenging and sometimes lonely journeys of trying to unpack data and connecting numbers to practical ways of supporting multilingual learners in daily instruction. This book is based on research-based practices and is designed as a fun but goal-oriented travel companion that is sure to stop and smell the roses along the way. Filled with colorful graphics that make reading easy and content comprehensible, this book is created with multilingual learners' success in mind. The collaborative assessment guide was created with the collaboration of the two phenomenal authors at its best!

—Dr. Inna Slisher, English Language Learners Supervisor,
Knox County Schools, TN

One of the book's unique strengths lies in its emphasis on leveraging the combined knowledge of educators, students, and families. This collaborative approach, presented through an engaging 'journey' theme, equips teachers with practical strategies to seamlessly integrate assessment into daily routines. This minimizes disruption while maximizing learning opportunities. The book's clear and accessible presentation makes it easy for educators to grasp the concepts and readily apply them in their classrooms.

—Dr. Lynn Shafer Willner, Standards and Accessibility Researcher/Digitalization Specialist,
WIDA at the University of Wisconsin-Madison, WI

Margo Gottlieb and Andrea Honigsfeld, renowned for their expertise in assessment and collaboration, show us how to support multilingual learners' language, academic, and social-emotional development using state-of-the-art collaborative assessment practices. Whether you are new to teaching or a veteran educator, this book should be front and center for building student success.

—Dr. Debbie Zacarian, Founder, Zacarian and Associates LLC, MA

Collaborative Assessment for Multilingual Learners and Teachers

Dedication

We dedicate this book to all the wonderful educators we have met throughout the years with whom we have collaborated on our educational journeys across the nation and around the globe.

Collaborative Assessment for Multilingual Learners and Teachers

Pathways to Partnerships

Margo Gottlieb

Andrea Honigsfeld

Foreword by Maria G. Dove

Illustrations by Claribel González

FOR INFORMATION:

Corwin
A SAGE Company
2455 Teller Road
Thousand Oaks, California 91320
(800) 233-9936
www.corwin.com

SAGE Publications Ltd.
1 Oliver's Yard
55 City Road
London EC1Y 1SP
United Kingdom

SAGE Publications India Pvt. Ltd.
Unit No 323-333, Third Floor, F-Block
International Trade Tower Nehru Place
New Delhi 110 019
India

SAGE Publications Asia-Pacific Pte. Ltd.
18 Cross Street #10-10/11/12
China Square Central
Singapore 048423

Vice President and Editorial Director: Monica Eckman
Acquisitions Editor: Megan Bedell
Content Development Editor: Mia Rodriguez
Content Development Manager: Lucas Scheicher
Senior Editorial Assistant: Natalie Delpino
Project Editor: Amy Schroller
Copy Editor: Karin Rathert
Typesetter: C&M Digitals (P) Ltd.
Cover Designer: Gail Buschman
Marketing Manager: Melissa Duclos

Printed in the United States of America

ISBN 9781071930861

This book is printed on acid-free paper.

24 25 26 27 28 10 9 8 7 6 5 4 3 2 1

Contents

Companion Website Contents

Please visit the companion website for downloadable versions of the resources listed above.
https://companion.corwin.com/courses/CollaborativeAssessmentMLT

Foreword

In over forty years of working in and observing PreK–12 classes, I have found a modest number of teachers who systematically incorporate classroom assessment, analyze and extract the data students produce, and use the data to refine on-the-spot or future lessons or scaffold instruction for those students who require additional support. Moreover, even fewer teachers share their assessment practices or data with one another. Without an organized process for collaboratively developing assessment or analyzing and sharing the data, many schools, especially those serving multilingual learners, risk keeping students in a cycle of underachievement across academic disciplines and fall short in developing their language and literacy abilities.

Using a siloed approach to teaching, twentieth-century teachers generally worked in isolation to develop lessons, deliver instruction, create assessment, and evaluate student work. In contrast, the demands of twenty-first-century curricula—critical thinking, problem solving, information analysis, media literacy, facility with technology, and so on—necessitate a more collaborative system for planning, teaching, and assessment. Twenty-first-century skills require collective expertise, varied perspectives, and multilevel feedback from diverse educators. The importance of teacher collaboration becomes even more pronounced when considering the educational needs of multilingual learners, and collaborative development and review of assessment practices have never been more crucial to student success.

When teachers partner, they are better able to tailor assessment that is not only accessible for multilingual learners but also linguistically and culturally responsive, ensuring that each assessment measures what was intended without ambiguity or bias. Through shared insights and observations, teachers who work together develop a more holistic view of student progress, moving beyond traditional systems of measurement, such as test scores or grades, and considering a broader range of factors that contribute to students' overall development. A collaborative approach to assessment enables the creation and implementation of targeted instruction that can be finely tuned to each learner's trajectory toward language proficiency and content attainment.

Coassessment is an essential part of the collaborative instructional cycle—planning, instruction, assessment, and reflection. It plays a pivotal role by promoting a shared understanding among teachers of the unique challenges of multilingual learners. Through coassessment, teachers collaboratively review students' work, fostering a more inclusive perspective on multilingual learners' content and language development. By developing a system for collaborative assessment, teachers can not only identify students' areas of strength and challenge them more effectively but also exchange ideas and strategies, enriching professional growth and fine-tuning instructional practices. Ultimately, coassessment fosters a shared responsibility among all teachers for the education of multilingual learners.

In *Collaborative Assessment for Multilingual Learners and Teachers: Pathways to Partnerships*, Margo Gottlieb and Andrea Honigsfeld provide a critical framework for educators to partner together to organize, examine, and evaluate student work to enhance lesson planning and instructional delivery for multilingual learners. They provide a priority map for the hierarchy within school organizations to initiate and sustain collaborative practices and guide their readers through the sometimes complex yet practical aspects of coassessment across disciplines. Through case studies and real-world examples, the authors illustrate how collaborative assessment can lead to more meaningful and equitable educational experiences for multilingual learners, foster their academic success and linguistic development, and promote a culturally responsive approach to assessment practices. This comprehensive book provides invaluable resources for teachers to effectively meet the diverse challenges of assessment for multilingual learners while guiding the collaborative efforts of teaching partners. By offering practical guidance and insightful frameworks, strategies, and tools, the authors empower teachers to amplify their assessment practices and deepen collaboration within their school communities.

As you read this book, you will uncover how to begin or continue on your collaborative assessment journey. You will develop an understanding of assessment—AS, FOR, and OF learning—to enhance collaborative and instructional practices, such as how to support students to reflect on their own learning together, how to coconstruct learning targets and success criteria with students, and how to go about evaluating students' completed work equitably and collaboratively. Additionally, you will learn techniques for leveraging collaborative assessment to promote inclusivity and fairness, ensuring that every student's voice is heard and valued in the evaluation process.

Collaborative Assessment for Multilingual Learners and Teachers: Pathways to Partnerships offers a deep dive into the tools and techniques available for fostering collaborative assessment practices. It presents a diverse array of assessment strategies designed for educators, as well as peer evaluation protocols that promote student engagement in reflective conversations about their learning. The book outlines specific techniques for observing student teamwork and using classroom observation protocols to collect essential insights. By providing a structured approach to implementing collaborative assessment practices effectively, this book incorporates multiple opportunities for readers to pause and reflect, inviting readers to consider ideas on their own as well as discuss them with their teaching partners.

Collaborative assessment of student work reflects a broad shift in education to focus on inclusivity and equity for all learners. By coassessing student work, teachers recognize the unique requisites for the success of multilingual learners as well as how to develop assessment that promotes opportunities for their learning and growth. Collaborative assessment is essential to ensure fair and accessible assessment, promote students' abilities to reflect on their learning, and provide all students with equitable opportunities to demonstrate their knowledge and skills.

—Maria G. Dove

Acknowledgments

First, we would like to thank our editor, Dan Alpert, for his decades of work at Corwin Press, during which time he urged us to interweave collaboration and classroom assessment practices, strengthening the impact of both. Dan has been an unparalleled champion of equity and critical friend with a staunch vision. In addition, we wish to express our gratitude to the entire Corwin team, especially Megan Bedell, who has assumed Dan's leadership as acquisitions editor. Mia Rodriguez, content development editor, Lucas Schleicher, content development manager, and Natalie Delpino, senior editorial assistant, have been helpful in the manuscript preparation and production process as has Amy Schroller, our project editor. A round of thanks also goes to Melissa Duclos, marketing manager, who has spearheaded the book's marketing campaign. Every book requires attending to a million details, and it is always a pleasure to know that conscientious eyes have reviewed all its fine points, including Karin Rathert, our copyeditor.

A huge thank-you goes to our colleague, friend, and collaborator, Maria G. Dove, for offering her insightful foreword. The artistic talents of Claribel González are prominent throughout the book, and we thank her for the creative icons and sketch notes that lead you down the trails of our journey. In addition, we would like to thank Kelsey Marci for her technical assistance with organizing the many citations and references and Sherry Liptak for her assistance with the final readthough of the page proofs.

The collaborative assessment stories from all the educators sprinkled throughout the chapters bring the book to life and hopefully help you, the reader, gain insight into the possible for your classrooms, schools, and districts. From small towns to large cities, around the United States and abroad, we are grateful to you for lending your collective voices to this book (in alphabetical order): Jill Ayabei, Shanel Barrett, Kelli D. Bernedo, Samantha Blanks-Gonzales, Fara Musser Blaszak, Catherine Raines Bura, Tamara J. Coburn, Kelly Cray, Andrea Dell'Olio, Rebecca Gerding, Ceci Gomez-Galvez, Jackie Griffin, Kimberly Henry, Stephanie Just, Kathleen Kemme, Christine Kennedy, Sara Klaahsen, Victoria Lore, Lindsay Manzella, Jessica Marty, Cindy McGean, Alexis Kiana Ortega, Alycia Owen, Alma Pezo, Molly A. Riddle, Ashley Rovner, and Jane Russell Valezy. We are very fortunate to feature so many unique examples representing different pathways to collaborative assessment across classrooms, schools, networks, and districts in K–12 settings.

About the Authors

Margo Gottlieb, PhD, has always been a staunch advocate for multilingual learners and their teachers. As cofounder and lead developer of WIDA at the University of Wisconsin-Madison in 2003, Margo has helped design and contributed to all the editions of WIDA's English and Spanish language development standards frameworks and their derivative products, including the Can Do Descriptors and *Essential Actions*. Starting her career as a Chicago Public Schools teacher, Margo worked with multilingual learners and their families; as director of assessment and evaluation at the Illinois Resource Center, she shared her expertise with educators. Being a bilingual teacher, facilitator, consultant, teacher educator, and mentor across K–20 settings, she has worked with universities, organizations, governments, states, school districts, networks, and schools in coconstructing linguistically and culturally sustainable curriculum and reconceptualizing classroom assessment policies and practices.

Margo's passion has always been assessment in its many forms, starting with her dissertation, a K–12 multilingual test in Spanish, Lao, and English that integrated content and language. Since then, she was appointed to national and state advisory boards, served as a Fulbright Senior Scholar in Chile, and was honored by the TESOL International Association in 2016 for her significant contribution to the field. In her travels, Margo has enjoyed keynoting and presenting across the United States and in 25 countries. Having authored, coauthored, or coedited over 100 publications, including 20 books and guides, Margo's third edition of her best-selling book, *Assessing Multilingual Learners: Bridges to Empowerment* (2024), is the latest addition to her Corwin compendium.

Andrea Honigsfeld, EdD, is a professor in the School of Education at Molloy College, Rockville Centre, New York. Before entering the field of teacher education, she was an English-as-a-foreign-language teacher in Hungary (Grades 5–8 and adult) and an English-as-a-second-language teacher in New York City (Grades K–3 and adult). She also taught Hungarian at New York University. She was the recipient of a doctoral fellowship at St. John's University, New York, where she conducted research on individualized instruction and learning styles. She has published extensively on working with English language learners and providing individualized instruction based on learning style preferences. She received a Fulbright Award to lecture in Iceland in the fall of 2002. In the past twelve years, she has been presenting at conferences across the United States, Great Britain, Denmark, Sweden, the Philippines, and the United Arab Emirates.

She coauthored *Differentiated Instruction for At-Risk Students* (2009) and coedited the five-volume *Breaking the Mold of Education* series (2010–2013), published by Rowman and Littlefield. She is also the coauthor of *Core Instructional Routines: Go-To Structures for Effective Literacy Teaching, K–5 and 6–12* (2014) and *Growing Language and Literacy* (2019, 2024) published by Heinemann. With Maria Dove, she coedited *Coteaching and Other Collaborative Practices in the EFL/ESL Classroom: Rationale, Research, Reflections, and Recommendations* (2012) and coauthored *Collaboration and Co-Teaching: Strategies for English Learners* (2010), *Common Core for the Not-So-Common Learner, Grades K–5: English Language Arts Strategies* (2013), *Common Core for the Not-So-Common Learner, Grades 6–12: English Language Arts Strategies* (2013), *Beyond Core Expectations: A Schoolwide Framework for Serving the Not-So-Common Learner* (2014), *Collaboration and Co-Teaching: A Leader's Guide* (2015), *Co-Teaching for English Learners: A Guide to Collaborative Planning, Instruction, Assessment, and Reflection* (2018), *Collaborating for English Learners: A Foundational Guide to Integrated Practices* (2019), and *Co-Planning: 5 Essential Practices to Integrate Curriculum and Instruction for English Learners* (2022). She is a contributing author of *Breaking Down the Wall: Essential Shifts for English Learner Success* (2020), *From Equity Insights to Action* (2021), and *Digital-Age Teaching for English Learners* (2022). Ten of her Corwin books are bestsellers.

About the Illustrator

Claribel González is a resource specialist for the Regional Bilingual Education Resource Network (RBERN) in western New York. She supports districts in achieving academic excellence for multilingual learners through professional development, technical assistance, and instructional coaching. Her passion for language and equity started at a young age as she was raised in a bilingual home and experienced the benefits of participating in bilingual programs. As an avid doodler, she celebrates creativity and the power of sketch notes as a vehicle to synthesize information. She has illustrated *From Equity Insights to Action: Critical Strategies for Teaching Multilingual Learners* (2021) and *Co-Planning: Five Essential Practices to Integrate Curriculum and Instruction for English Learners* (2021), both published by Corwin. González has served as a bilingual classroom teacher and district instructional coach. She is currently a doctoral student in the language education and multilingualism program at the University at Buffalo. Her research interests include bilingual education, biliteracy, and assessments.

Setting Out on a Journey Through Collaborative Assessment

1

The essence of education is not to transfer knowledge; it is to guide the learning process, to put responsibility for study in the student's own hands, and place people on their own path of discovery and invention.

—Tsunesaburo Makiguchi

Are you ready to join us on an extraordinary trip? Are you excited to explore some new territories with us? We definitely are! We have been preparing for this journey for quite some time, so we are thrilled you are here with us!

After many years of following each other's work, at long last we, Margo and Andrea, met in person during a retreat organized by our publisher, Corwin, and began to toss around the idea of collaborating one day. As with many educational partnerships, developing a deep understanding of each other's professional stance generally takes time. At first, there were many competing demands, but over the years, we couldn't help but notice how often we kept crossing paths. At long last, we were able to collaborate!

As we traveled around the United States and beyond, we frequently found ourselves in the same professional space. We participated in some of the same online events during the COVID-19 pandemic, and ever since those trying times, we have cowritten a chapter, served on a panel discussion, participated in joint webinars, and copresented at conferences.

As we kept running into each other—in person or virtually—and our professional lives kept intersecting, we were delighted to rediscover our shared professional interests, including our joint passion for collaboration as the heart of relationship building.

So here we are—our first coauthored book, which we envision as a journey with stops along the way to capture our paths of discovery and on-going learning metaphorically. Each chapter represents a significant adventure we invite you to embark on with us. Throughout the book, "we" will refer to us (Margo and Andrea) as authors, and "you" will address either the readers of the book directly or educators of multilingual learners.

What Is This Book About?

This K–12 practical guide is designed to provide you with ready-to-use tips and adaptable templates that streamline the assessment process and embed it into everyday classroom routines. Set within an assets-based approach to learning, we showcase how collaborative assessment practices support multilingual learners' academic, linguistic, cultural, and social-emotional development. We share evidence-based, research-informed strategies for successful classroom implementation.

Countering the challenges from overreliance on data from high-stakes tests for accountability purposes, we pose pedagogies designed around multilingual learners' linguistic and cultural resources. Through numerous authentic examples, we show meaningful and actionable ways to collaboratively examine student learning within *instructional* and *assessment* cycles across grade levels and content areas.

We highlight how content teachers, ELD or bilingual educators, and other specialists, when working together, can advance teaching and learning for multilingual learners. We also focus on how multilingual learners can interact with each other through dialogic inquiry in seeking responses to questions that they have generated. You will find evidence of how this overall trust built into classroom communities elevates the role of assessment in providing useful information for in-the-moment, short-term, and long-term decision-making.

Why Is This Book Needed?

The connection between learning and assessment is becoming much closer than ever before as educators take on a more active role and pay closer attention to multilingual learners' language and literacy development within content learning (Davison & Leung, 2012; Gottlieb & Katz, 2020). But you don't have to do it all and do it alone! The stage has been set for collaborative assessment that embraces increased student voice and choice in documenting their evidence for learning as well as teacher agency to take informed action based on students' needs. We also intend to illustrate the ease with which content and language teachers as well as multilingual learners and families can combine their expertise to ensure and promote linguistic and cultural equity in classroom assessment.

Let's start our journey around the United States and beyond by first by visiting Jackie Griffin, director of Curriculum, Professional Learning, and Language in Skokie School District 73, Illinois, who leads and supports collaborative assessment practices.

> *At East Prairie, multilingual learners are immersed in a dynamic coteaching environment where collaboration is at the forefront. EL teachers work hand in hand with general education classroom teachers, coplanning, coteaching, and coassessing to ensure seamless integration of language development with academic content. Within grade-level teams, teachers collaborate to identify students' mastery levels of standards, providing targeted support or extension as needed. EL teachers contribute a crucial language perspective to these*

discussions, offering valuable suggestions and scaffolds to empower multilingual learners and all students to reach their full potential. This collaborative approach fosters an inclusive and supportive learning community where every learner is equipped with the tools they need to succeed. (See Figure 1.1.)

Figure 1.1 A Road Map of Collaborative Assessment Practices in Skokie School District 73

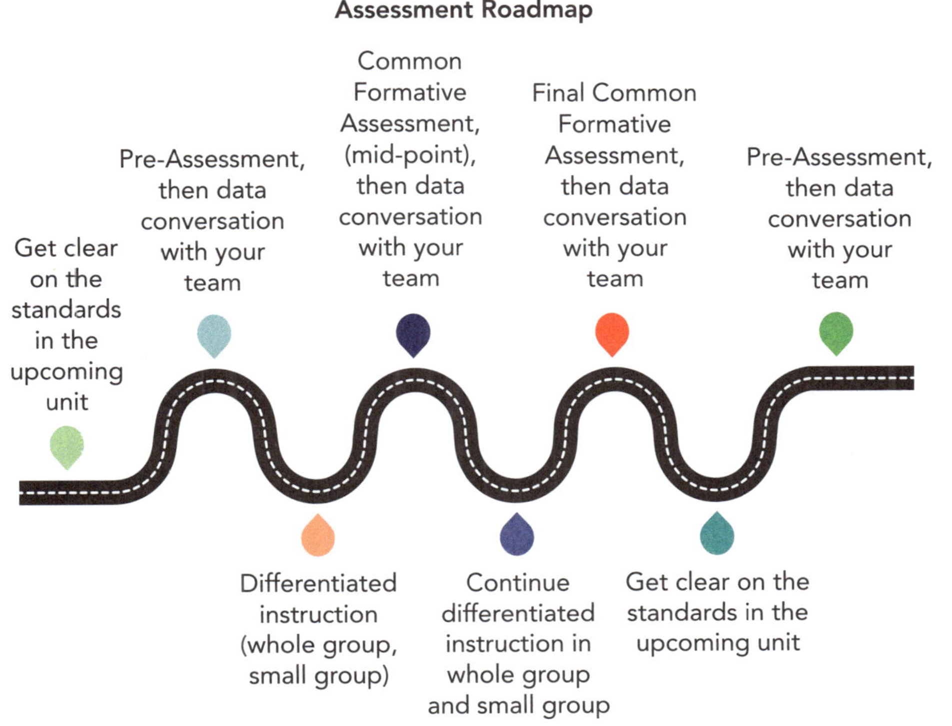

All districts and schools should have a road map that delineates their collaborative assessment journey. In that way, there is a clear vision of the destination and timeline. If not already in place, you should consider coconstructing a map of your own as you read through the chapters, getting feedback from colleagues, and amending it along the way.

Norms for Collaborative Instruction and Assessment

Seven core norms have informed our work and more specifically, have guided the writing of this book. They are based on the premise that in the classroom, collaborative instruction and assessment are intertwined and codependent, so much so, that the two are inseparable. Research-informed and evidence-based practices as well as our recommendations are systematically built upon them:

1. Assets-Based Pedagogy as the Norm

Rather than taking on a deficit-oriented perspective, putting labels on children, or ignoring the rich diversity that students bring to school from home, we fully embrace an assets-based approach to all aspects of multilingual learners' education.

Beatriz Arias (2022) reminds us that this type of "teaching requires that educators abandon a focus on the perceived limitations and weaknesses in students and expand their understanding of the strengths, assets, and funds of knowledge that students and their families possess" (p. 3). Since its inception in 2003, WIDA, a consortium of more than 40 states, territories, and federal agencies, has been dedicated to supporting educators of multilingual learners and has perpetuated a "can-do" philosophy as a primary value for fostering language development and learning (WIDA, 2019). Similarly, other states and Canada have moved into an advocacy role for promoting assets-based educational practices for multilingual learners.

2. Culturally and Linguistically Responsive and Sustaining Education as the Norm

Built on a long tradition of culturally relevant and responsive pedagogies (Gay, 2000; Ladson-Billings, 1995), we advocate for creating a student-centered learning environment inside and out of school that affirms all learners' cultural and multilingual identities, honors their ways of knowing based on their frames of reference, and consistently builds on students' strengths. "Culturally sustaining pedagogy seeks to perpetuate and foster—to sustain—linguistic, literate, and cultural pluralism as part of the democratic project of schooling" (Paris, 2012, p. 93).

3. Student Voice and Choice as the Norm

When classrooms and schools center students, their values, perspectives, passions, and interests become paramount in curriculum, instruction, and assessment. Additionally, for multilingual learners, their languages, cultures, and histories are reflected in their learning environment and classroom activities. When students have voice and choice, they become responsible for and agents of their own learning. "Incorporating student voice and/or family voice into student learning is a promising strategy for teachers striving to foster culturally responsive classrooms to enhance education access, opportunity, and success for students who are historically marginalized within the pre-kindergarten to grade 12 education systems" (IES REL Pacific, n.d.).

4. Multilingualism as the Norm

Many students come to school with a primary language other than English. Many more speak more than one language or dialect at home or in their local communities and communicate with immediate or extended family members engaging in fluid, dynamic *languaging*—"the process of making meaning and shaping knowledge and experience through language" (Swain, 2006, p. 98). Multilingual learners also hold onto a critical dimension of their identities, self-definition, and self-expression through language (Esteban-Guitart & Moll, 2014). We strongly agree that language rights are human rights and knowing more than one language is a superpower (see USDOE, 2023). Multilingualism is an ambitious expectation we have for all students and educators both as an individual commitment and societal norm.

5. Learner Variability as the Norm

There is a vast diversity within any group of learners when it comes to their prior and current learning experiences, their motivation and abilities, and their talents, gifts, and interests. Most multilingual learners are uniquely positioned to be at the intersection of sociocultural, academic, cognitive, and linguistic experiences: Our responsibility as educators is to provide them with equitable access to culturally and linguistically responsive and sustaining curriculum, instruction, and assessment through highly engaging and relevant learning experiences. Acknowledging the variability of student characteristics, learning situations, and teacher preparation, research suggests an increase in the likelihood of multilingual learners' success when favorable conditions are created for the following: (a) climate for learning, (b) challenge as learning, (c) clarity of learning, (d) cohesion in learning, and (e) checks into learning (Fisher & Frey, 2023).

6. Family Engagement as the Norm

Multilingual learners, as all children, come from rich family traditions and complex historical, cultural, and individual experiences. Families of students who have been historically marginalized need to see schools as institutions to trust and educators as partners. To achieve this, we advocate for collaborative strengths-based family engagement rather than 'involvement' at its core; we recognize families and their languages, cultures, and traditions as important contributors to students' educational experiences that are integral to schools' curricular journeys.

To tap family expertise and bring it into the fold of schooling, Louise El Yaafouri (2019) offers six tips to encourage their successful engagement. They include the following: (1) making engagement reciprocal by establishing a partnership between family members and the school, (2) aiming for authenticity by "championing relationship building through collaboration" (para. 6), (3) using a culturally responsive approach, (4) keeping it simple through clarity of communication, (5) increasing capacity in growing family members as leaders, and (6) finding your way home through home visits.

7. Collaboration as the Norm

Teaching is a complex profession that requires educators to share their expertise, combine their knowledge and skills, and create shared goals with viable pathways to their success. By forming and engaging in vibrant communities of practice, all stakeholders recognize the challenges and opportunities of working with diverse student populations who deserve nothing less than a shared ownership of equitable, joyful, and enriching learning experiences. What starts with occasional dialogue between students, students and teachers, or among educators hopefully expands to sustained ongoing collaborative action. As Tamara J. Coburn, lead ESL teacher in the Winston-Salem/Forsyth County Schools, North Carolina observes: "Change happens in conversation before it can happen in the classroom."

How Is the Book Organized?

To make this book reader-friendly, we wanted to keep it relatively short and accessible; thus, we have six interconnected chapters filled with figures and icons to lead the way. The following chapter summaries give you a preview of what you will find in each chapter and how we have planned this journey for you:

Chapter 1: Setting Out on a Journey Through Collaborative Assessment

This introductory chapter frames our book. It articulates the context, defines the goals for writing this book, and sets the tone for our travels. We identify the purpose and the foundation for our work and establish its focus in support of multilingual learners. In providing a rationale for collaborative assessment and its advantages for advancing teaching and learning, we set the course for establishing a must-read guide for educators who wish to coordinate instruction and classroom assessment for multilingual learners.

Chapter 2: Collaborative Instructional and Assessment Cycles

In this chapter, we briefly introduce two codependent cycles. The first, the collaborative instructional cycle, consists of four interrelated components: collaborative planning, instruction, assessment, and reflection. We show how together, the four components maximize teacher effectiveness and impact multilingual learners' language and literacy development, content attainment, and social-emotional growth. Within the instructional cycle, we introduce the second cycle, the five iterative phases of assessment, from planning to taking action; we then elaborate how each phase dovetails with and reinforces instruction. Finally, we preview the content of the next three chapters—assessment AS, FOR and OF learning—and how it fits into the collaborative instructional and assessment cycles.

Chapter 3: Collaborative Assessment AS Learning

Building multilingual learners' metalinguistic, metacognitive, and metacultural awareness is integral to collaborative assessment AS learning as it sensitizes multilingual learners to different facets of self-reflection as part of their identity formation. This extension of assessment AS learning invites multilingual learners to learn from each other and form strong and lasting relationships. Simultaneously, it taps the students' linguistic and cultural resources and their use of translanguaging as a collaborative instructional and assessment strategy. We illustrate how students can gain agency in becoming personally accountable for learning and the drivers in setting personal goals, monitoring their own learning, and celebrating their successes.

Chapter 4: Collaborative Assessment FOR Learning

In this chapter, we highlight how students and educators develop relationships by collaborating in classroom assessment. We illustrate how students, in conjunction with their content and language teachers, participate in the instructional and assessment cycles. We learn how students, along with teachers and coaches, determine the best options for multilingual learners and how teachers, counselors, and multilingual learners explore course options based on information from multiple assessments. In assessment FOR learning, we offer opportunities for you and your students to codesign integrated learning goals and targets and learn how, together, you both benefit by giving and receiving feedback.

Chapter 5: Collaborative Assessment OF Learning

Collaborative assessment OF learning entails a broad range of measures, from those in individual classrooms to ones mandated by the state. With representation from all stakeholder groups, we see the emergence of student, teacher, and leader agency as a road to empowerment. Through student-led conferences and different forms of teacher facilitated project-based learning, we see how students and teachers form partnerships in deciding multimodal evidence for learning. In essence, this chapter shows you how data from assessment OF learning complement those of assessment AS and FOR learning to build and fortify a collaborative system where multilingual learners and their teachers have active roles.

Chapter 6: Collaborative Assessment Beyond the Classroom

The final chapter goes beyond the day-to-day in-class practices of assessment AS, FOR, and OF learning and invites you to build partnerships with a range of educators and service providers, coaches, leaders, and families. We continue to urge all members of your school community to take a multilingual turn (May, 2014) and adhere to multiliteracies as principled pathways to student success. We illustrate how our collaborative assessment framework that is anchored in multilingual learners' and their families' linguistic and cultural assets can be adopted school- and districtwide. We also advocate for a systemic approach to collaboration, with a special emphasis on coassessment. The book closes with signs of hope for advancing collaborative assessment as the *overriding norm* in classroom and school settings.

What Are Some Recurring Features?

The chapter summaries might have given you the impression of a book that reads like an academic text. Fear not! We meant it when we suggested early on that we are taking you on a journey. (We don't want to overpromise . . . but this might just end up being a journey of a lifetime!) There are several unique, recurring features in each chapter to serve as your navigational tools and signposts. Our intention is to keep guiding you through the journey of topic exploration while also providing you with continuity and stimulating learning experiences.

We have woven the travel metaphor throughout the book with each chapter unfolding as a different place along our journey. You will notice that the section headings and subheadings as well as the colorful icons created by Claribel González all suggest different aspects of our travels. The major headings are presented in a question format, whereas the subheadings give suggestions or suggested action steps for your consideration.

Where Are We Going?

We launch each chapter with a brief visit to the sprawling Katherine Johnson campus with its elementary, middle, and high school. As each section opening question suggests, we want you to get oriented to the topic of the chapter by meeting different educator teams and witnessing a typical scenario or conversation that takes place on campus. The vignettes offer a unique context for each chapter while making the content readily accessible and relatable.

There are two subsections here to aid in our exploration; first, under **Finding Our Way**, we elaborate on the introductory vignette, and then under **Considering Our Options**, we offer alternatives or extensions to our discussion that you may wish to pursue.

How Will We Get There?

The purpose of the next major section is to establish the goals of the chapter and, just as a GPS does, to map out possible routes to follow.

Why Is/Are [________] Important in Our Journey?

The first thing you might notice in the section heading is that there is a placeholder; it indicates that the title is going to change based on the topic we are exploring. Here our aim is to establish a rationale for the chapter and make a strong case for our recommendations. In that way, you can readily communicate the vision of and the know-how for collaborative assessment to others.

Under **Educator Promises,** you will find a brief introduction followed by a list of promises associated with collaborative assessment practices between students, students and teachers, and teachers that we hope you also embrace. These promises relate our hopes for multilingual learners and their teachers in enacting the instructional and assessment cycles.

How Should We Prepare for ________?

Before we set out on a journey, we need to be well informed and well prepared, so we usually hop on the internet and search for some information. In this section, we offer a detailed description of the topic (where we fill in the blank) and we address what is entailed in classroom implementation.

What Are Some Caveats/Challenges Along the Way?

We do not shy away from obstacles and roadblocks, nor do we want to pretend that there are no unforeseen difficulties along the way. So here we discuss the challenges that we have observed—and you can anticipate—connected to the topic of the chapter. We also offer suggestions for how you might circumvent some of the warning signs.

What Do We Need to Pack?

The journey we are taking you on requires careful preparation and lots of tools and techniques. Here we present practical strategies and resources that you can readily adopt or adapt to your own local needs and contexts. Additionally, we share some resources we hope you find useful in your collaborative assessment journey.

Periodically throughout the chapters, we employ two additional features to reinforce the concepts we introduce.

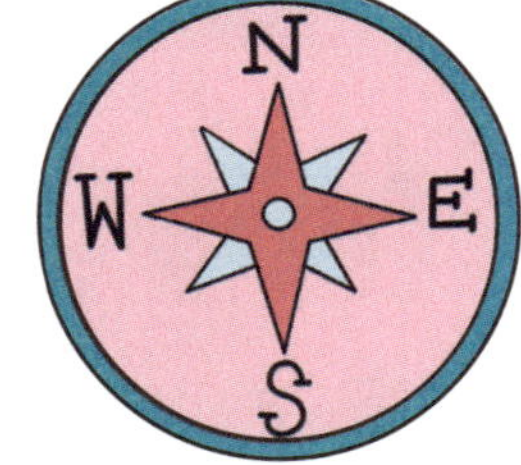

The first, the compass, reminds us of the importance of relying on research and evidence-based best practices. Look for the inserts where we present key research findings or citations that further support our claims and guide our thinking,

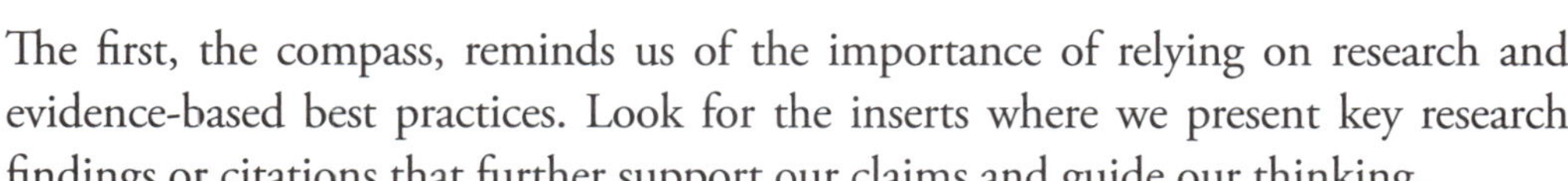

The second additional feature, the pit stop icon, invites you to take a short break on your journey with us, process the information we have presented, and reflect on its relevance, usefulness, and applicability to your own context.

Which Pathways Should We Take?

When we travel, we often find many roads in front of us; at times, perhaps, it may seem as if there are even too many paths to choose from! In this section, we recognize and present alternative choices for collaborative assessment as you follow the topic at hand. Here our intent is to guide you and your students in making the most appropriate decisions in choosing the trails you wish to take.

What Should We Do Before Leaving This Stop?

When seeing this icon, you are ready to look back to where you have been on this journey and think back on your successes (and challenges). As we wrap up the chapter, we summarize the key take-aways so you are not too bogged down with luggage.

Where Do We Go Next?

As we head toward our destination, we ask you to slow down a bit. In the final major section of each chapter, we prompt you with some questions to reflect on what you have discovered, determine your own next steps, or plan some new directions to take with colleagues and others, including multilingual learners.

In addition to these recurring features, in each chapter, we take side trips to visit educators around the United States and internationally to learn about their collaborative instructional and assessment practices. We appreciate the trust these educators have placed in us, and we are thrilled to have this unique opportunity to share their experiences with you. You will learn first-hand what works for whom, and why, how, and what kinds of locally developed assessment tools and protocols they have implemented in supporting assessment for multilingual learners.

Introducing the Katherine Johnson Campus

As we begin our journey, we invite you to take a tour of the Katherine Johnson campus with us. "Where is this place and why are we going there?"—you might wonder! This campus, with its three connected schools, is the location of the introductory scenarios that launch each chapter. Through these composite vignettes, we tell the story of many schools, campuses, and districts around the country that are working toward advancing teaching and learning through collaborative assessment for their growing populations of multilingual learners.

The Johnson campus is part of an urban district, but we recognize that many of its practices and policies also have applicability to schools in suburban and rural settings. Its leadership has worked particularly hard to have community outreach to ensure organizations and agencies are integrated into its welcoming culture. Students and families are welcome to access all the multilingual services and contribute their expertise, such as suggesting different classes and taking the initiative to form different clubs.

We realize that this campus is unique in its comprehensiveness, serving as a hub for the entire community. In particular, classes at Johnson include technology, culture workshops, yoga and tai chi taught by family members, as well as courses in three languages, English, Spanish, and Vietnamese. The campus also welcomes local youth clubs, offers meeting space for some youth and community-based organizations, houses several sports teams, and has recently fulfilled the community's desire for a health clinic.

There are even more highlights! The campus has reciprocity with the local library: Teachers share print and digital resources, they intentionally build a joint collection in multiple languages with input from multiple stakeholders; consequently, the library offers afterschool homework help, tutoring, and enrichment programs. Some campus activities are only available to families or caregivers of children attending the schools to encourage and support their engagement. Other events are open to the public, including student performances, concerts, and a recently launched speaker series that focuses on topics families have requested in multiple languages: healthy nutrition, family literacy, digital citizenship, financial literacy, and language development.

You can see why community building is important for the Katherine Johnson campus—unfortunately, we don't have space to elaborate on it in this book. However, we wish to underscore that the campus serves as the heart of the community. The leadership's intention is for everyone to feel safe and welcome in their schools and surroundings. In addition, secondary students are encouraged to complete their service-learning requirements for graduation within the campus and community—for example, by mentoring students in younger grades or helping the elderly or homebound.

You might be wondering about the demographics of this vibrant community. The campus has close to 40% of its students receiving language support services. There are cotaught language development and content classes as well as a recently established two-way Spanish–English dual language program available to students. More than 15 other languages and cultures are sprinkled throughout the campus, and the multilingual hallways and classroom spaces are a testament to valuing the multiculturalism of the student body. Most importantly, the lived experiences of the students have been systematically embedded within the linguistically and culturally sustainable curriculum.

Let's hear from some educators at the Johnson campus who will share their experiences about an on-going initiative to make learning experiences more consistent, better coordinated, and more impactful for multilingual learners across the various programs.

Ms. Álvarez, the principal of the elementary school, offers the larger campuswide context to the *Collaborative Instructional Assessment Initiative* that is highlighted in the book's scenarios:

> *As a school community, we have been very intentional about introducing and systematically supporting this initiative to support our multilingual learners. As one of the pilot schools in the district, we have been participating in a three-year plan. Year 1 focused on collaborative planning and Year 2 on collaborative teaching (prioritizing coteaching but also being flexible to include coordinated or partnership teaching, consultative teaching, and language- and literacy-focused coaching). Now we are in Year 3, and while we continue to strengthen the previous two years' implementation goals, we are focusing on embedding collaborative assessment into curriculum and instruction.*

Ms. Bentley, an early elementary grade team leader, reflects on the initiative:

> *I really appreciate how we have regularly scheduled coplanning time. In Year 1, it was a bit random at first, but by Year 2, we pretty much had it down. We have learned a lot: We share our beliefs about multilingualism and our resources, such as recommended articles, blogs, and books we find on early childhood education specific to multilingual learners. This year, all grade-level teams informally compare notes about their multilingual learners, exchanging their documentation of student growth toward meeting grade-level standards. To the extent feasible, we always include students in the process.*

Mr. Pongrácz is a middle-school educator with multiple certification areas, elementary (with a middle school extension in English language arts), special education (K–8), and an endorsement in K–12 English language development:

> *As a seasoned educator, it was quite an adjustment for me to work more closely with the sixth-grade team. For many years, I was a middle-school self-contained special education teacher. Yes, I was one of those naysayers or fence-sitters—my colleagues teased me about this a lot, but they also listened to my concerns and took my suggestions seriously. Now it makes sense for all of us to work together to create more cohesion! Plus, I no longer feel that I need to know and do it all. . . . that's what colleagues are for . . . to share the responsibility for teaching our multilingual learners.*

Mr. Ciano is the Grade 6 through 8 English language development teacher who travels from class to class:

> *This is what I love about this year: Previously, we had done a lot of work with curriculum mapping and aligning content standards to language and literacy development goals. We started this year by coming together to understand who our students are and what they can do, and we did this work from a whole new perspective. We are expected to examine and interpret data before we come to our weekly meetings! We bring student work samples as evidence of their progress, and we talk a lot about and with our students. We make sense of the data together as everybody sees what the students can do a bit differently.*

Ms. Delva, a paraprofessional and bilingual family liaison, is striving to become a bilingual teacher:

> *I feel my input is welcome and appreciated this year more than in the past. I have been a para working in the district for several years. I am almost finished with my BA in early childhood education, and I am learning so much in the college classroom and even more from my colleagues at school. This initiative has helped me realize that I know a lot about the students and their families. I have been observing these students and connecting with them and their families using our shared languages (I am fluent both in Spanish and Haitian Creole). I have learned that I can offer unique and valuable insights into what the students are experiencing out of school or what they are feeling and thinking when they are lost or overwhelmed. I am also excited to serve as the school bilingual family liaison, which is something I have been doing informally but now it is official, and my families love it!*

Mr. Attali takes pride in being a language development coach:

> *I am new to this role, and am very proud that the district established some new positions in pilot schools. I got selected after many years of serving in a range of capacities, including an ELD teaching assistant, bilingual teacher, and dual language educator. My responsibility is to take on a nonjudgmental, nonevaluative role in listening to challenges teachers face and facilitating collaborative processes to help them cogenerate possible solutions on behalf of their multilingual learners.*

Ms. Young, the district technology coordinator, is constantly being challenged by her growing responsibilities:

> *My role has evolved over the years from offering simple tech support, mainly purchasing equipment and uploading or updating software, to creating a digital ecosystem for the campus. Since COVID, we have been issuing a Chromebook to each student and a laptop to every teacher with a range of programs that are incorporated into sustained in-house professional development. We feel that access to assistive technology as well as multilingual resources [and] translation and interpretation tools are critical for equity across the campus.*
>
> *This year we have implemented a new data tracking system so teachers can share information about their students, collect and store evidence of student learning digitally, document student growth, and better communicate with caregivers and families. Our next challenge is to collaborate on a new policy to address generative AI (artificial intelligence) in the classroom, for the school, and beyond. We continue to learn about AI and expand technology in the district to stay current and pedagogically sound. I might be the district coordinator—however, I work with a team, and it really takes a combined effort to cocreate policy to move the campus forward.*

You might have guessed—yes, there are many more members of the team at the Katherine Johnson complex! While we want to acknowledge all stakeholders, this short introduction through the voices of collaborating educators gives you a feel for the ongoing shift and sense of community that defines the campus. In each subsequent chapter, you will meet a different grade-level team so you can experience a cross-section of collaborative practices across the campus.

How Might This Book Guide You in Supporting Multilingual Learners?

Our hope is that by the time you complete this journey with us, you will have experienced professional affirmation and also will have developed a deeper understanding of how collaborative assessment can create pathways to success for multilingual learners as they interact with each other, other students, and teachers. We will have tackled issues related to assessment literacy and offered you templates for enhancing classroom assessment practices and cocreating assessment policy for multilingual learners. Whatever your position, we will have always tried to center multilingual learners throughout the collaborative instructional and assessment process (Gottlieb, 2022a).

You should not have to work in isolation. Instead, in reading this book, we would like you to envision how you can access strategies that establish or enhance student engagement and agency in collaborative assessment. As professional learning communities or communities of practice, we hope you will have opportunities to process the information, try out some of the protocols, and apply or adjust them to your own contexts.

Let's take a quick detour to Hazelwood School District north of St. Louis, Missouri, where Jessica Marty, coordinator of English Learner, Immigrant, and Migrant Education Services, has been leading a similar change in assessment practices for years:

> *In response to inconsistencies in grading practices for multilingual students, the Department of English Learner, Immigrant, and Migrant Education Services in Hazelwood School District embarked on what has become a transformative journey toward collaborative assessment within its coteaching initiative. Over the past six years, we have made significant strides toward shaping a comprehensive collaborative assessment framework. Collaborative grading now ensures that each student, in accordance with their individualized language plan (ILP), receives assignments and grades aligned with their English proficiency level, fostering an equitable learning experience.*
>
> *From kindergarten to high school, technology-assisted collaborative assessment ensures timely feedback for both multilingual and non-multilingual students. This shift from disjointed practices to coassessment has not only resulted in more equitable grading but has also improved student performance on classroom assessments. Through in-the-moment conversations and shared grading efforts, coteachers facilitate meaningful collaboration, ensuring that assessments are not just a measure but a road map for success.*

So, Are You Ready to Join Us?

Pack your bags and prepare for this trip with us as we explore the stops ahead! Whether you are traveling solo, bringing some of your colleagues along for a joint adventure, or recruiting your entire school community for this expedition, this journey will expand your horizon, take you to some more or less familiar territories, and offer some breathtaking views of the range of assessment approaches along the way. We're excited to invite you along with us as we proceed to our first stop of our journey, the collaborative instructional and assessment cycles. Together, in partnership, let's forge new pathways as we partake in our adventure.

Collaborative Instructional and Assessment Cycles 2

Collaborative practice [is] a complex and dynamic social process where individuals interpret the situation and navigate multiple competing influences.

—Lindy L. Turnbull and Susan M. Carr

Where Are We Going?

The First Stop on Our Journey: A Team Meeting

Since the inception of the *Collaborative Instructional Assessment Initiative* two years ago, the Katherine Johnson campus with its elementary, middle, and high schools has incrementally embraced a team approach to planning instruction for *all* learners. There is no more of a "*my kids, your kids*" mindset among the faculty as the last two years have shown how critical it is to have a shared commitment to equity with access and opportunity for every student.

The campus has grown to learn that it is paramount to articulate a clear vision of community along with collaboration *and* to enact it daily. Students, educators, and the families all know that belonging comes first because the success of each child's academic, language, and social emotional development depends on their combined efforts (Berryman & Eley, 2019). How do teachers show that teaching and learning are a joint endeavor? One way they do so is by creating a welcoming school and classroom community; preparing learning experiences every day that affirm students' cultures and languages, nurture students' curiosity and challenge them to learn, build trusting partnerships with fellow educators, and support each other as colleagues on this journey.

Finding Our Way

At the beginning of each year, Katherine Johnson educators come together to work through a protocol to better understand who their students are, what they can do, and how to plan instruction based on information from students and their evidence of learning. Let's listen to a snippet of the seventh-grade team's conversation as they collaboratively look at data from the first few weeks of school to design instruction and classroom assessment.

Ms. Evans, the seventh-grade lead teacher: Does everyone have their first [Google] folder open where the student roster has been coded for multilingual learners' language proficiency and additional services? As most of us have classes with multilingual learners who span from newcomers to those born and raised in the community, that information is tremendously helpful. In today's meeting, we are going to share the information from the students' individual portraits as we coplan for coteaching and coassessment for this first quarter.

Sra. Martínez: The portraits are always a "work-in-progress" that our students update throughout the year. I have most of the family data for my class, so I'll be happy to team with the students later today.

Ms. Tren: Most of my students have finished their self-portraits. As an opening activity, I asked them to complete a figure of their heads, putting their interests and passions on the right side and the goals they set for themselves on the left. By next week, I can come back with a class summary of all the students' talents and gifts.

Enlarge this diagram and follow the directions in the box.

On the right side (the artistic half): What are your interests? What are your passions or hobbies?

On the left side (the analytic half): What are your in- and out-of-school goals for this year? Which subject(s) and topics do you like to explore and why?

Ms. Evans: Thanks, that's great. Do you think we should also collate the student-set goals? While I want to focus on individual needs and understand how students perceive themselves, it might be helpful to see the big picture for the seventh grade regarding the types of goals and student aspirations.

Mr. Shapiro: Definitely! When we plan our upcoming unit for learning, we can tap into those goals.

Ms. Tren: Let's take a look at the initial student-generated data we have from last week.

[The team discussion continues with *looking back* at data and *looking ahead* to planning the next unit with student interests and lived experiences in mind.]

Having initial impressions of their students' likes and ambitions, each grade-level or department team throughout the Katherine Johnson campus next tackles their planning protocol (see Figure 2.1) for collecting information for instruction and assessment. The shared commitments among team members to continue the collaborative assessment journey are heartwarming. Teams have an understanding that they will follow the agreed-upon steps and engage in rich conversations guided by questions for coassessment as part of the coplanning process.

Figure 2.1 An Evidence-Based Coassessment Planning Protocol

STEPS IN INITIAL DATA COLLECTION AND ANALYSIS	KEY QUESTIONS TO ASK OURSELVES
1. Collect evidence for student learning based on agreed-upon learning targets	• How are we assessing both content attainment and language development of our multilingual learners?
2. Organize data and prepare for collaborative discussions	• How do we know that our students are successful?
3. Identify patterns in student learning	• What trends are emerging for different groups of students?
4. Align student needs and interests to upcoming unit goals	• How do we coplan to ensure all students are growing and making progress? • Have we attended to our students' characteristics, including their languages, cultures, and experiences?

The four steps for data collection and analysis along with the guiding questions in Figure 2.1 are an example of engaging in evidence-based collaborative conversations. There are other ways that you can establish an instruction and assessment protocol. As you take some time at this pit stop, reflect on and discuss the following:

- What are important data-related questions for you and your team?
- What classroom instruction and assessment routines or protocols have you tried in the past? Which ones worked and why?
- Which classroom instruction and assessment routines or protocols needed adjustment, and how were adjustments made?
- How did the data from instruction and assessment routines or protocols contribute to related decisions or policies?

You probably noticed the close proximity of instruction and assessment in the protocol. That's because collaborative instruction and classroom assessment are often seamless, becoming intermingled during implementation. That's one of the purposes for taking this journey—to show you how collaboration permeates and binds instruction and assessment.

Collaborative conversations—as illustrated by discussions spurred by the protocol—are an initial step in preparing for our adventure into the world of collaborative classroom assessment. We will explore how sustained teacher collaboration leads to more coordinated intentional learning experiences for all students and their subsequent documentation of learning. Ultimately, we hope to witness how teacher dedication to and advocacy for their students results in equity and excellence across classrooms and schools.

Considering Our Options

To create a system of support for an integrated instructional model for multilingual learners, the Katherine Johnson leadership team, with district support, established collaboration as a campus-wide signature pedagogy. Focus group discussions and surveys helped map out some essential aligned components at the district, school, and classroom levels (see Figure 2.2).

Figure 2.2 A Sample Priority Map for Establishing and Sustaining Collaboration Across Levels of Implementation

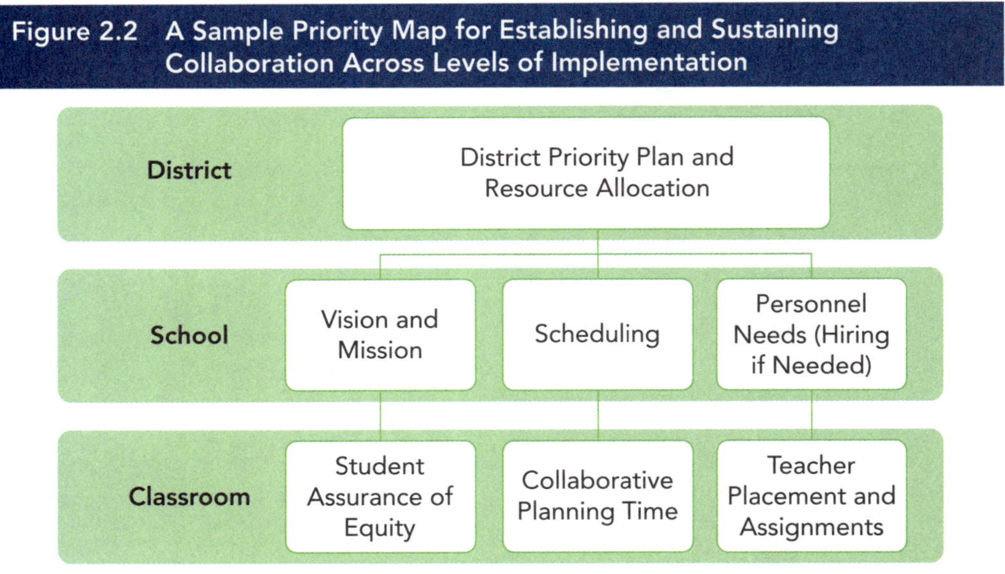

We understand that at any given time, there are always multiple (and often competing) initiatives taking place in districts and schools. To illustrate our point, we have gathered up the demands (and opportunities) for educators across the Johnson campus. Some new initiatives are simultaneously being rolled out while others have a longer history and are currently in later stages of implementation. When educators ask, What else can you put on my plate? we encourage them not to consider collaboration another initiative but rather a way of school life that is nurtured by teachers holding their hands up (see Figure 2.3).

Figure 2.3 Collaboration for Districtwide Initiatives

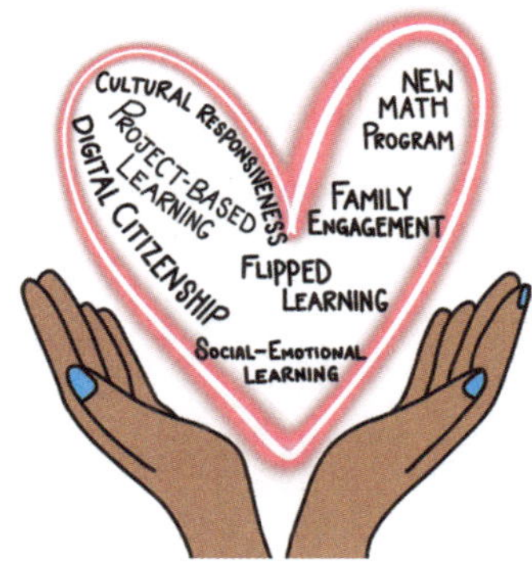

How Will We Get There?

With Clarity and Purpose!

In this chapter, we briefly introduce (or reintroduce) the collaborative instructional cycle consisting of four interrelated components:

1. Planning
2. Instruction
3. Assessment
4. Reflection

We show how all four components implemented cyclically maximize teacher effectiveness and impact multilingual learners' language and literacy development, content attainment, and social-emotional growth. We then connect the collaborative instructional cycle with the five phases of the assessment cycle (see Figure 2.5). Finally, we preview how the content of the next three chapters—assessment AS, FOR, and OF learning—fits into the collaborative instructional and assessment cycles.

Why Are Collaborative Assessment Practices Important in Our Journey?

It's Our Mission!

The knowledge base on collaborative inclusive or integrated practices for multilingual learners as well as for students with exceptionalities has been expanding in the past decade (Auslander & Yip, 2022; Cohan et al., 2020; Friend & Cook, 2016; Honigsfeld & Dove, 2021; Murawski & Lochner, 2017; Villa et al., 2013; Yoon, 2022). Like many researchers of inclusive multilingual education and practitioners working collaboratively in schools, we advocate for

- Taking a systemic approach to initiating an integrated model of instruction that includes collaborative partnerships, grade-level instructional teams, school and district administrators, and instructional coaches (Auslander & Yip, 2022; Jenkins & Murawski, 2024)
- Creating the conditions in which all participating teachers engage in a cycle of collaboration, including coplanning, coteaching, coassessment, and reflection (Dove & Honigsfeld, 2018; Honigsfeld & Dove, 2019, 2022)

- Building capacity for collaboration through collaboration (Nordmeyer & Honigsfeld, 2023)
- Planning on incremental implementation with periodic quality reviews and revisions to the implementation plan (Dove & Honigsfeld, 2020)
- Mapping out classroom assessment practices with students that are synchronized with instructional practices (Gottlieb, 2024)
- Ensuring that students have voice and choice during instruction and assessment (Gottlieb, 2021, 2022b)

Educator Promises for Collaboration

Creating an integrated collaborative framework for instruction and assessment requires a cogenerative process that helps develop shared understanding, joint professional learning, and intentional pedagogy for all learners. As you embark on your journey with us, we ask that as an educator of multilingual learners, you do the following:

- You and your colleagues define and refine what collaboration is and what it looks, sounds, and feels like in your context.
- You and your colleagues identify and utilize the assets and accessibility of multilingual learners so they, too, can equitably participate in all learning experiences.
- You and your colleagues commit to schoolwide long-term collaborative practices in support of multilingual learners through instruction and assessment.
- You and your colleagues forge professional partnerships to design and implement instructional and assessment practices with more consistency and continuity.
- You and your colleagues analyze and interpret student evidence for learning and discuss your findings.
- You and your colleagues engage in on-going reflection, dialog, and decision-making as you contemplate and evaluate the relationship between collaborative instruction and assessment.

Let's visit Alma Pezo, assistant director of multilingual education, and her colleagues in Chelsea Public Schools, Massachusetts, where the multilingual education (MLE) team has created a collaborative assessment protocol inspired by the Consultancy Protocol (Center for Leadership and Educational Equity, n.d.). Alma not only shared the purpose, the group norms, and the protocol with us, but she also shared a carefully crafted tool to help capture participating educators' thoughts about student learning.

Purpose

We work together to . . .

- *Leverage our collective knowledge and expertise to identify high-impact instructional practices/strategies to help our students meet their language growth target and master necessary academic language, knowledge, and skills*
- *Build our MLE team capacity and collective efficacy to look closely at evidence of student academic language use and engage in rich, productive dialog about learning and teaching*

Norms

- *We use asset-based language and focus on what students CAN DO.*
- *We stay focused on things YOU (WE) can influence, impact, change and improve.*
- *We honor the protocol. The purpose of the protocol is to provide structure, safety, predictability, and equity of all voices.*

See Figure 2.4 for a note-catcher developed by Alma's team with reminders of the purpose of each step of their protocol, the time allocated to complete each step, and select guiding questions:

Figure 2.4 Example of a Collaborative Assessment Protocol

TASK, STANDARDS, AND ACADEMIC LANGUAGE EXPECTATIONS	
Step 1: Describe the student, the task, the standards, and the academic language focus (1–2 mins) • *Why did you select that particular student to focus on?* • *What strategies have you tried so far?* • *What are you hoping to get help with for this student?*	
STEP 2: Others ask clarifying questions about the student, task, WIDA English Language Development standards, and academic language (1–2 mins)	
STEP 3: Presenter shares evidence of student learning: things a student CAN DO at this time in relation to the standards and task along with things that student is challenged by (3 mins) *What evidence of the standards do you see in the student work?* • *At this time, the student is able to . . .* • *The student is not able to . . . YET*	
STEP 4: Partner/Others ask probing questions about the student; try hard to avoid suggestions (2 mins) • *What approaches have been the most impactful so far?* • *In your opinion, what is the most important challenge for the student for growing in this area?*	

(Continued)

(Continued)

TASK, STANDARD, AND ACADEMIC LANGUAGE EXPECTATIONS	
STEP 5: Discuss the strategies and possible next steps **The presenter "steps out of the circle" and ONLY listens and takes notes (5 mins)** • *Something you might try is . . .* • *I wonder if . . .*	
STEP 6: Presenter decides on the next step(s) (2 mins) • *After our conversation, I plan to . . . because . . .* • *I am planning to monitor the student's language growth by . . .*	
STEP 7: Both partners reflect (1 min) • *What did this conversation make you think about in terms of your own practice?* • *Based on our conversation, something I can take away and apply in my own practice is . . .*	

Used with permission.

How Should We Prepare for Collaborative Instructional and Assessment Practices?

By Building Partnerships!

Collaboration during instruction and classroom assessment might help you expedite our journey although it might not be the norm in many schools (yet). So we invite you to "log into your search engine" and ask yourselves the following questions:

- What is already in place and successful for your multilingual learners?
- What have your multilingual learners contributed to the collaborative conversation?
- How can looking through the lens of your multilingual learners enhance effectiveness and impact of collaboration?
- What should be designed and incrementally rolled out with clarity and intention?

Examine the Collaborative Instructional Cycle

For successfully designing, implementing, and continually improving a collaborative pedagogy in serving multilingual learners, teacher teams must make a commitment to attend to the instructional cycle (coplanning, coinstruction, coassessment, and coreflection) and think about how we might embed phases of the assessment cycle. Although our book is on collaborative assessment practices, we recognize that no one component of collaborative cycles ever happens in a vacuum.

Let's start by introducing (or for some of you, revisiting) the components of the collaborative instruction cycle, defining each one, and offering some compelling arguments for engaging in each for multilingual learners. Also, you may notice what the four members of the seventh-grade team from our chapter opening vignette say about the past two years of their collaborative instructional assessment initiative.

The Four Components of the Collaborative Instruction Cycle

1. **Collaborative planning**

   Coplanning is most frequently focused on a joint effort between teachers to implement a standards-aligned curriculum and differentiate instruction within a unit of study or lesson to address all students' varied strengths and needs. During designated coplanning times, you should rely on each other's expertise and resources to accomplish the following:

   - Establish learning targets and instructional/assessment procedures for reaching those targets
   - Integrate the academic content and language development of all learners
   - Provide students with multiple opportunities to practice language and content-specific language with multimodal support
   - Determine appropriate modifications and adaptations to teaching
   - Agree on embedded classroom assessment tools and procedures to inform instruction

Ms. Evans:

I see how collaborative planning connects to coassessment—since planning is based on evidence for student learning and figuring out where students go next—to inform instructional decisions.

2. **Collaborative instruction**

   Collaborative instructional practices may take place as a codelivery of instruction by two or more educators in the same classroom space or as a carefully coordinated, aligned teaching practice offered by several collaborating educators. As a member of a partnership, you may assume multiple, changing roles to motivate and challenge every student in your classroom during instruction.

Mr. Shapiro:

Multilingual learners require consistency and continuity, clear expectations, and rigorous well-supported instruction. When we coordinate our instruction, whether through coteaching or partnership teaching, we can seamlessly embed assessment so that students know up front ***where*** *they are going,* ***what*** *evidence to produce, and* ***which*** *options to choose from.*

3. **Collaborative assessment**

   Collaborative assessment is a cyclical process unto itself that dovetails with collaborative instruction. Each time new data are collected, students' progress and performance are reevaluated. Reflecting on your students' academic learning as well as their language, literacy, and social-emotional development, you can then plan accordingly, often with input from the students themselves.

Sra. Martínez:

Teachers in our school bring different areas of expertise and perspectives to the assessment process, just like our students! We always learn from looking at student work together.

4. **Collaborative reflection**

   Shared reflection on student and teacher learning may end or begin the collaborative instructional cycle. It creates opportunities for you to acknowledge and examine the challenges you face and celebrate your multilingual learners' successes.

Ms. Tren:

Initially, I thought, "How are we going to have time to reflect when there is barely enough coplanning time? Now that we have routines and protocols, I see how, as collaborative educators, we must stop and think deeply both about our own practice and its impact on student learning.

When you share and discuss the components of the collaborative instructional cycle with other educators, you intentionally focus on the whole student and their content, language, literacy, and social-emotional development!

Let's take a side trip to visit Jill Ayabei, in West Ada School District, Idaho, who is the district K–12 multilingual coteaching specialist/grant coordinator and has recently offered her perspective on the collaborative instructional cycle with a focus on coassessment:

> *A complete collaborative instructional cycle promises success to teachers working together for multilingual learners. When a content teacher and an ML teacher take the time to plan, teach, assess, and reflect together, MLs get the full support they need. Too often, teachers have limited time to reflect about their teaching and their students' learning, but when they can do this, especially together, they are able to focus on what the students know, what they still need to know, and how the teachers can help them get there. When both teachers have input in each part of the cycle, a fuller picture emerges of the students and their learning.*
>
> *Teachers who collaborate on student assessment gain a richer, more comprehensive perspective than they would individually. This collaborative approach allows them to analyze assessment from various angles, resulting in increased clarity for the teachers and their students. Content teachers, for instance, examine assessment through a broader informational lens, considering students' learning of content. Meanwhile, ML teachers focus on language to ensure comprehension. By collaboratively addressing what students need to know and how they can demonstrate their knowledge, teachers help students access content through language. This approach, involving backward planning and coassessment, benefits all students. Additionally, including students in defining their end goals, learning objectives, and methods of demonstration helps deepen their learning process. Although teacher collaboration demands more time, reflection, and intentionality, the ultimate outcomes justify the investment.*

The collaborative instructional cycle—as its name suggests—is cyclical by design with recurring components, and it is most often presented with collaborative planning as the first step. We wish to recognize that this cycle is dynamic and multidirectional because we *collaboratively* work on the following:

- Cocreating learner portraits and using the information throughout the cycle
- Identifying students' strengths, talents, gifts, and areas of need
- Determining students' eligibility to receive language and academic support services
- Using data to place students in the most appropriate setting and design instruction so that students can thrive
- Noticing students' moment-to-moment, day-to-day, and week-to-week progress
- Evaluating students' progress over time.

Figure 2.5 identifies and describes the components of the collaborative instructional cycle with a colorful spinner in the middle. What is that you might ask? It is a reminder that *the five phases of assessment* (represented by the five colors of the spinner) are connected to and embedded in the four components of the collaborative cycle.

Figure 2.5 Integrating the Collaborative Instructional and Assessment Cycles

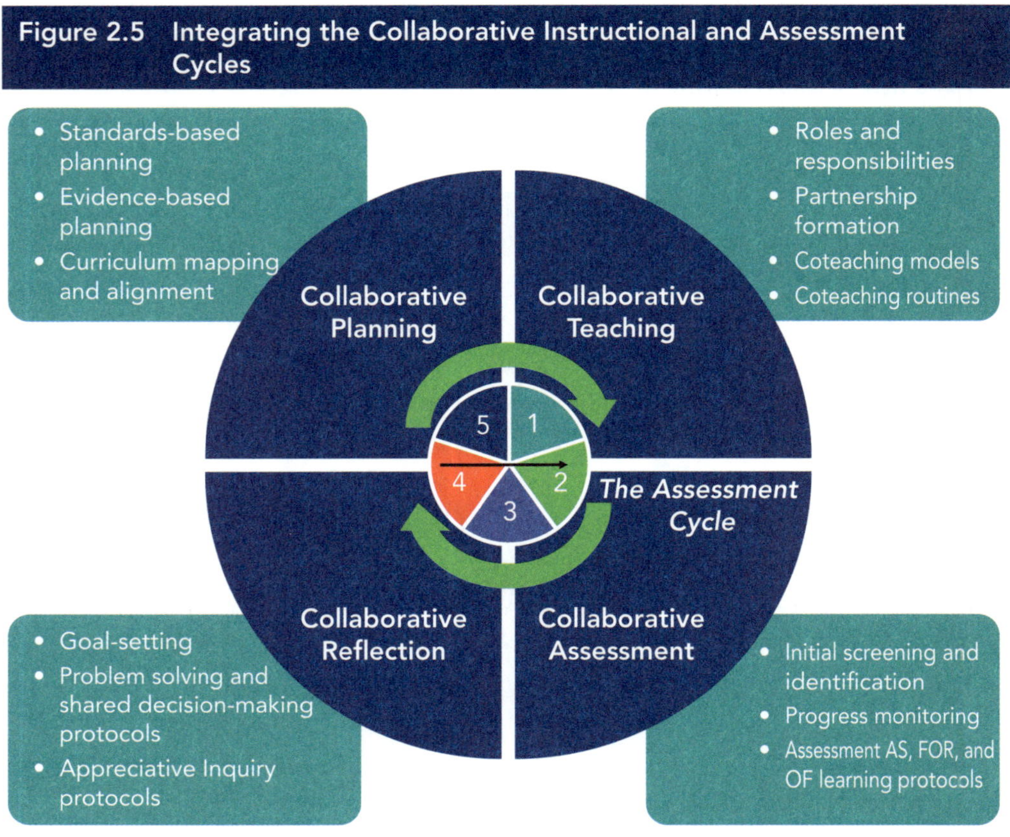

Embrace the Assessment Cycle

As the three schools enter Year 3 of the Collaborative Instructional Assessment Initiative, the Katherine Johnson campus uses the concentric circles of collaborative instruction and assessment as their compass. Being well versed in the collaborative instructional cycle, educators now spend time superimposing the assessment cycle onto it to coordinate their classroom activities.

With coplanning as the North Star in the journey for both instruction and assessment, we briefly describe the five phases of the assessment cycle that are internal to collaborative instruction. Let's also hear from other members of the Johnson campus introduced in Chapter 1 and illustrated in Figure 2.6.

Figure 2.6 Envisioning the Assessment Cycle Within the Collaborative Instructional Cycle

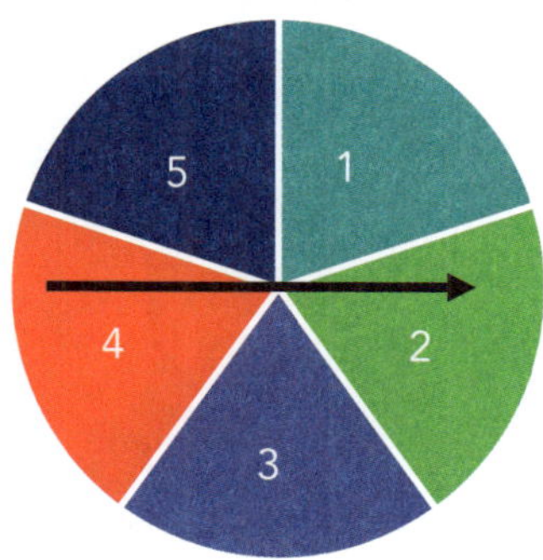

The Five Phases of Collaborative Assessment

1. **Planning assessment in one or more languages**

   "Where do we even begin?" you might ask. For units of learning (and assessment OF learning), you and your team, whether a grade-level or a professional learning community, should create an overall goal and an accompanying student-informed or student-generated project, product, or performance. Coplanning with your students should extend (in assessment FOR learning) to coconstructing learning targets for individual lessons that lead to the unit's project. Within individual lessons, students should interact with each other and reflect on their learning (in assessment AS learning).

Ms. Bentley, an early elementary grade team leader:

Let's make sure that our learning goals for our units and their corresponding learning targets for our lessons are coordinated. Our students should act as decision-makers, specifying what they are to accomplish (during instruction) and agreeing on evidence for learning (for assessment). In that way, instruction and assessment are collaborative, complementary, and seamlessly interwoven.

2. **Collecting and organizing assessment information**

   Once the learning goal and targets are in place, your next decision is "*What* kinds of information will we associate with each assessment approach, AS, FOR, and OF learning, and *who* is going to participate in each approach, students, students and teachers, and teachers with input from students?"

Mr. Attali, the language development coach:

If we are to agree on the information we are going to collect for assessment purposes, we first have to think about what is available to us for our multilingual learners. Let's brainstorm what we need to consider to contextualize and better understand our data, for example:

- *The learning goal or target that specifies the unit's or lesson's overall purpose*
- *The language(s) of instruction and assessment*
- *The mode(s) of communication (interpretive [listening, reading, viewing] and/or expressive [speaking, writing, representing])*
- *Additional modalities available for evidence (e.g., oral, audio, graphic, kinesthetic)*
- *Other resources (e.g., technology)*

What else might impact the information we gather for assessment?

3. **Interpreting assessment information and providing feedback**

   How do you and your students decide what the information from assessment means and how might you be able to offer concrete objective advice as to next steps? Referencing the unit's goal for learning or lesson-level learning targets, to make sense of student data, you should think about the

   - Students and their individual characteristics
   - Presence of linguistic, cultural, gender, experiential, or religious bias
   - Content and language demands of the project, task, or activity
   - Time and preparation required by the teachers and students
   - Ways to give concrete actionable feedback

You should also be aware of what interpreting assessment data does not mean. You should try to *avoid*

- Weighting what students produce (e.g., in terms of grading)
- Determining scores
- Tallying quantities
- Assigning letters to the quality of work (e.g., A–F)
- Using check marks (check plus, check, check minus)
- Giving phrasal feedback (e.g., Good job! or Well done!)

Ms. Delva, the paraprofessional and bilingual family liaison:

There is so much to remember, and often I have to translate all the information and make it understandable to families! Many families are not familiar with the educational system here in the United States, so I also must explain how it's different from the one that they do know. On top of it, families have children sprinkled throughout the three schools. Although classrooms are trying to reach consensus on how to interpret assessment information, uniformity across the campus has not yet been reached. We still could benefit from ongoing professional learning for everyone and together, develop an agreed upon policy.

4. **Evaluating and reporting assessment information**

   In this phase of assessment, students and teachers place a "value" on what has been accomplished. Thinking about the ways in which the information reflects the purpose for assessment and how the information is to be used, you may ask the following:

   - Do the results of students' efforts give answers to the question, Why assess?
   - How does this assessment project, task, or activity inform instruction?
   - Are the ways in which we report the information meaningful for our multilingual learners and multilingual learners with identified exceptionalities?
   - Based on what we have gleaned from assessment, how might students show agency?

Ms. Álvarez, the elementary school principal:

We have to be careful when we evaluate assessment information that we are not being judgmental about our students. Rather, we should make sure that when we report the results from assessment they are

- *Reflective of the unit's theme and referenced to selected standards*
- *Representative of learning goals (for units) and learning targets (for lessons)*
- *Understandable and useful for our students (and families)*
- *Assets based, accentuating the accomplishments of our students*
- *Timely, leading to additional learning opportunities for our students*

In addition, you and your colleagues should think about how to present assessment information to other audiences. There are quite a few options for reporting, including the following:

- Summarizing information by looping back to and revisiting student portraits
- Graphing student growth along with a narrative explanation
- Offering personalized descriptive feedback to individual students either orally or in writing
- Noting how far down the road the students have reached toward meeting designated academic content and language development standards (Gottlieb, 2022a)

5. **Taking action based on assessment results**

   What do we do in the last phase of collaborative assessment? Classroom assessment results can range from narratives to checklists to rubrics to some form of grading. There is a lot of assessment information, from everyday classroom assessment to annual testing, so how do you know what to focus on? That's where collaboration comes into play!

   The number one priority for you and your students should be examining the evidence for learning in relation to the overall grade-level learning goals. Then, you should determine your overall instructional plan based on those goals. You might take action by collaborating with your team or professional learning community, such as by engaging in research or contributing to policy. Other kinds of action might involve making connections between your classroom and your students' families or brainstorming with students how to build relationships among the classroom, school, and community.

Mr. Pongrácz:

Being a middle school teacher, I work with Mr. Ciano, the language development teacher, to better understand my multilingual learners' progress; in that way, we can coplan next steps. It's also advantageous for me to seek the advice of Ms. Young, the technology coordinator, to identify the criteria for helping my students and I select entries to store on the school's server. Many of my students are technology experts, and I can certainly learn from them! For example, I will ask my students how we might set up a system for scanning and uploading their work samples and evidence to their folders.

Different forms of assessment offer different types of data or information. Both you and your students should act based on the results from each form, whether from state annual tests, interim district measures, common school or grade-level prompts and projects, or everyday classroom activities. As the lion's share of classroom assessment is an everyday occurrence, students should have a voice in recommending the actions to take in figuring out their next steps for learning.

How might you configure the collaborative instructional and assessment cycles so they work in tandem and are meaningful to you? How might you and your grade-level, department team, or even your entire school agree on how to portray the strong partnership between instruction and classroom assessment?

Further Explore the Collaborative Assessment Cycle

In classrooms, the five phases of the collaborative assessment cycle work in conjunction with the collaborative instructional cycle. Centering multilingual learners, the multi-phased assessment cycle is dynamic and flexible, ranging from instantaneous or contingent actions to an activity within a lesson to pre-established times for undertaking common multi-grade assessment tasks. You should keep in mind another attribute of the assessment cycle—its inclusivity—with the aim of forming, nurturing, and maintaining relationships, including those with students, between students and teachers, and among educators with input from students.

Relationship building and these interactions are the basis for assessment AS, FOR, and OF learning, our collaborative model that is described in depth in the upcoming chapters. Figure 2.7 elaborates the five phases of the assessment cycle (as shown in the spinner in Figure 2.6), understanding their codependence with the components of collaborative instruction.

Figure 2.7

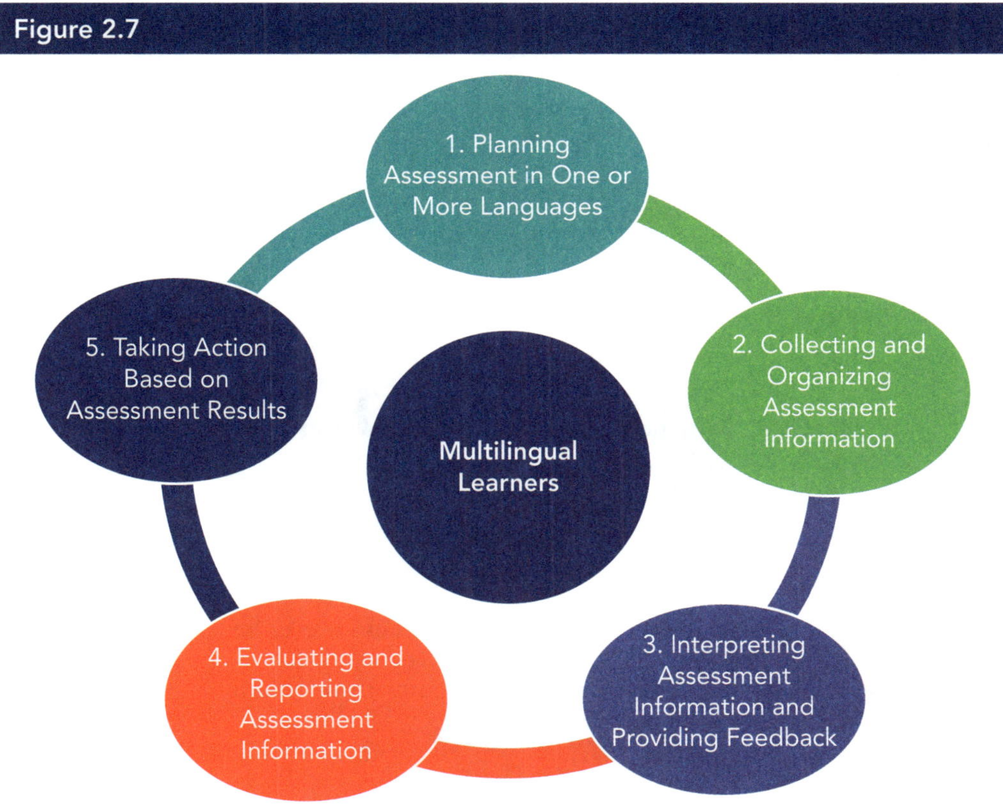

Gottlieb, 2021, 2022

By definition, multilingual learners are exposed to or have interacted in multiple languages and cultures; classroom assessment should always account for that fact in every phase of the assessment cycle (Gottlieb, 2021, 2022a). Thus, we begin coplanning assessment (Phase 1) alongside that for coinstruction, having a firm sense of each student's portrait, including their oracy, literacy, and conceptual development in English and their other language(s). For those of you who rely on backward design as a curricular framework, you should remember that classroom assessment is frontloaded in the instructional process so that we can always pinpoint our destination.

The remaining four assessment phases follow cyclically. They may be deliberate with built-in collaboration between students, students and teachers, or teachers; at times, they may be consolidated, occurring spontaneously within a lesson. The order of the phases may even be redirected or put on hold; for example, based on feedback, you may pause to take time for a mini lesson to clarify a concept or practice a specific language pattern in the context of content area instruction.

It is important to keep in mind that rigor never means simply assigning difficult work; instead, when multilingual learners are prepared for rigor, they understand themselves as contributing members of an academically rigorous, intellectually challenging school and classroom community. Students demonstrate an ability to use critical reasoning, take academic risks, and leverage a growth mindset to learn from mistakes.

—New York State Education Department (NYSED; 2019, p. 8)

What Are Some Caveats/Challenges Along the Way?

Don't Spin Out of Control With the Two Cycles!

The collaborative instructional and assessment cycles might strike you as orderly processes. But life is messy! Not everything goes neatly in order all the time; the cycles may not always be complete before you need to initiate a new one. While recognizing the fluidity and complexity of these processes, let's also agree as to what practices should be *avoided* as we pursue a new trail:

- The collaborative instructional cycle is not a one-way circular driveway: Its components are interconnected and continuously inform teachers' work.
- Collaborative assessment is not about creating or assigning new labels to students.
- Assessment is never a mystery, a gotcha, nor should it ever be used punitively.
- Assessment is not the same as grading, and conversely, grading is not the same as assessment.

- Assessment results should not lock students into static, rigid boxes and programs; rather, ongoing collaborative assessment should capture the dynamic, iterative nature of culturally and linguistically responsive teaching and learning.
- Assessment should not represent a single perspective that students must adhere to; rather, assessment should be framed with a multicultural lens.
- Assessment for multilingual learners should not be a paper and pencil (or digital) exercise or translation; collaborative classroom assessment should include resources and multimodalities that students can readily access in their multiple languages.

As you review our preceding short list of challenges, reflect on which of them describe your current or past experiences with your students. What other challenges exist in your context that we did not mention? What have you done or what do you plan to do to overcome or mediate those challenges?

What Do We Need to Pack?

Just the Right Amount!

When you pack your bag for a journey, you engage in at least two related processes: What to take and what *not* to take to avoid heavy luggage with unnecessary items that no one can lift or, worse yet, for which you may get charged extra on a plane.

Let's agree to actively prepare for our journey of collaboration by doing the following:

Making individual classroom and schoolwide commitments to collaboration

How to do it? By engaging in courageous, difficult conversations about collaboration and establishing clarity of expectations and norms

Building relational trust through the forging of professional partnerships

How to do it? By creating a culture of collaboration and entering into partnership agreements among leadership, teachers, students, and, to the extent feasible, families

Engaging in job-embedded professional learning experiences

How to do it? By participating in ongoing external and internal coaching, offering peer support, and engaging in intervisitations (teacher-to-teacher classroom observations)

Let's also agree what to intentionally *leave behind* in our travels:

- Preconceived notions or stereotypes about multilingual learners and their families
- Deficit-oriented approaches to teaching and assessment
- Excuses why we cannot work together more effectively or efficiently
- Fear of not knowing enough or not knowing it all—not speaking the students' home languages, not understanding the students' home cultures, not being certified in every content area
- Frustration with not doing or accomplishing enough
- Working with the assumption that there simply isn't enough time to accomplish what we are setting out to do
- Playing the blame and shame game
- Thinking that assessment has to be associated with grading
- Not giving students choices in instructional and assessment design, implementation, and evidence for learning
- Excluding students in decisions that directly impact them

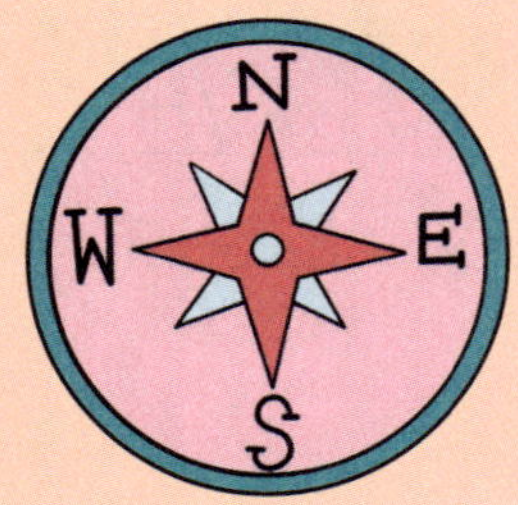

"Our attention to co-teacher relationships and practices is a critical step in promoting child-centered language development that affirms learners' identities."

—Stephanie C. Sanders-Smith and Liv T. Dávila (2021, p. 12)

Let's visit a a dual language elementary school (50% English, 50% Spanish), in North Shore School District 112, Illinois, where Stephanie Just, instructional coach, has found collaborative assessment to be an essential cornerstone of inclusive and effective instruction for multilingual learners.

> *A key aspect of our collaborative assessment protocol is the utilization of assessments in the first language of instruction. This initial evaluation enables us to comprehensively understand the academic and linguistic proficiency of our students. By leveraging assessments in the first instructional language, we gain valuable insights into individual strengths and areas for growth, which allows us to tailor our instruction appropriately to meet all of our students' needs.*
>
> *As we shift into the second language of instruction, collaborative analysis of assessment in this language allows us to transition and bridge from the first language of instruction. We are able to leverage students' strengths in*

the first language of instruction to build knowledge and skills in the second. Collaborative analysis throughout the second language of instruction is instrumental in gauging the progress of our students and allows us to integrate both language and academic scaffolds and support as needed. This approach ensures that our team's instructional strategies are responsive to all of our multilingual students' needs across both languages.

Are you ready for collaborative instruction and assessment to support multilingual learners? If so, you should adopt, if you haven't already, the following essential practices (see Figure 2.8).

Figure 2.8 Moves by Teachers and Coaches

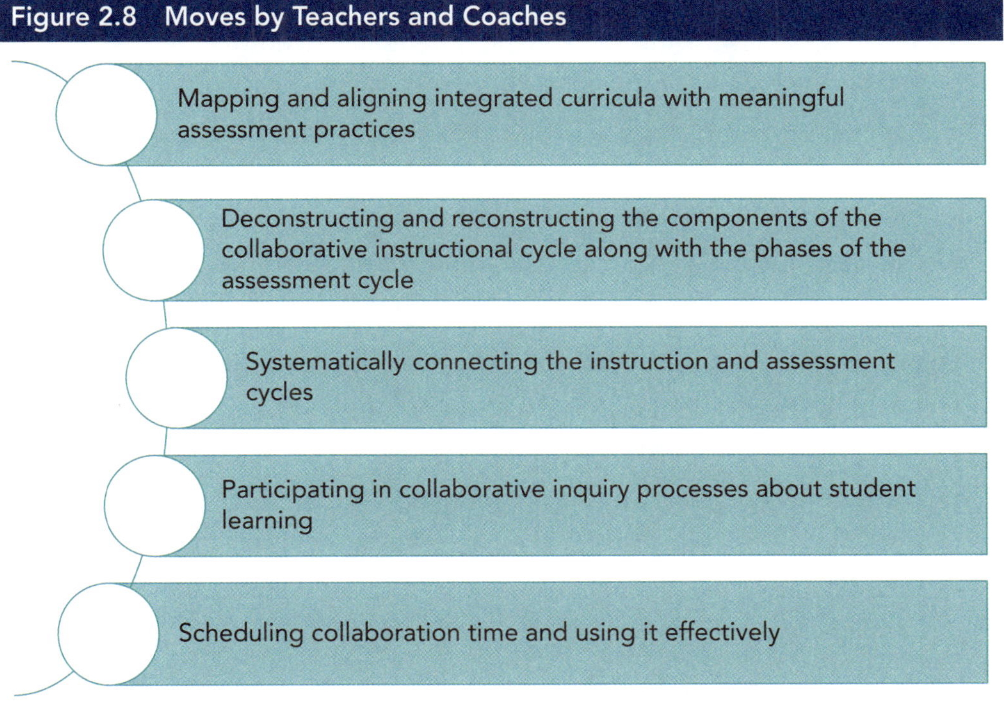

Focus on Day-to-Day Collaboration Strategies for Teachers

Here are some ideas to promote and maintain teacher collaboration:

1. **Start with what works well for you and your colleagues**

   When you operate from a strengths-based stance and start with successes, you will see what is possible and what is impactful, and you will be motivated to further both student and teacher learning.

   What Questions to Consider

   - What is in place already that is collaborative: Committees, grade-level team meetings, joint parent-teacher conferences?
   - Do you and your grade-level team participate in professional development and professional learning communities (PLCs) together?

- What time works for carving out collaboration?
- Do you coordinate the collection, analysis, and interpretation of student data with students and teachers during assessment AS, FOR, and OF learning?

2. **Continue to learn about your students' strengths and needs together with your colleagues**

   Be a champion for your students and avoid the road bumps or pitfalls of seeing deficiencies and noticing gaps rather than taking the time and collaborative effort to discover and advocate for student strengths.

   What to Focus On

   - Reflect on students' academic, language, and social-emotional development and make strategic short-term and long-term instructional and assessment decisions.
   - Shift conversations about what the students cannot do to what they have not mastered *yet*, what they are working on, what goals they have set for themselves, and how they plan to meet them.
   - Consider students' multilingual and multicultural identities and their strength of belonging.

3. **Engage in joint, sustained professional learning opportunities**

   - Establish "flexible teaming" that allows for both horizontal (on grade level) and vertical (across grade level) teacher teams.
   - Foster cross-disciplinary teamwork to support multilingual students' curricular, instructional, assessment, and extracurricular successes.
   - Establish inter-rater agreement among teachers on students' projects or samples based on a uniform set of descriptors.

   What You Share and Gain in the Process

   - Expertise of content, knowledge of literacy and language development, and pedagogy
   - Instructional and assessment resources, technology tools, and supplementary materials for students
   - Instructional and assessment strategies that represent research-informed and evidence-based best practices
   - Methods for coteaching and coassessing—ways to group students and optimize classroom space for student interaction during teaching and learning
   - A variety of perspectives or pathways to reach all students

4. **End with joint celebrations, shared reflections, and goal setting**

   - Invite students to participate in self- and peer reflection throughout the assessment process with a recap of successes.

- Exchange individual student and classroom accomplishments.
- Display original multimodal multilingual student work around the room and hallways.
- Have students contribute their thoughts and images to classroom and school websites.
- Coconstruct a standards-referenced protocol that accentuates what students can do.

Let's visit an international school in Vietnam, where homeroom and EAL teachers regularly coassess student work and at times, invite other members of the school community to garner diverse perspectives and build a common understanding of multilingual learners. In Figure 2.9, Denise Serna, Katie Rigney-Zimmerman, Stacey Preston, and Najela Blain-Hammond examine student work together.

Figure 2.9 Joint Exploration of Student Work to Ensure Multiple Viewpoints

Which Pathways Should We Take?

Study the Map to Figure Out Which Direction to Choose!

One of our core beliefs is all that we do in the classroom is driven by relationships and interactions. Assessment practices are no different. As suggested in our earlier work, "approaches to assessment are relationship driven, primarily among students (in assessment AS learning), teachers (in assessment FOR learning), and school leaders (in assessment OF learning)" (Gottlieb & Honigsfeld, 2020, p. 143). These three assessment approaches are described in Figure 2.10 with examples of collaborative practices and tools to collect and reflect on student data.

Figure 2.10 Summary of Assessment Approaches With Associated Teacher Actions and Example Tools

ASSESSMENT APPROACHES	COLLABORATIVE PRACTICES	EXAMPLE TOOLS
Assessment AS Learning	Inviting students to engage in self- and peer assessment Guiding students to self-monitor learning Encouraging students to take responsibility for their work and develop independence Helping students to document their growth and show evidence for learning Creating opportunities for peer feedback based on agreed-upon criteria for success Advancing students' learning by describing their own learning processes, strengths, and next steps	Utilized by students • Peer-editing checklists • Learning logs from different content areas • Interactive journals • Self-reflection tools
Assessment FOR Learning	Coconstructing success criteria with students carefully aligned to learning goals and targets Cocreating a menu of classroom assessment tasks that encourage student choice Determining assessment data collection methods within instruction Using data to give feedback to each other and plan/revise instruction	Utilized by students and teachers • Graphic organizers • Checklists • Templates for goal setting and criteria for success • Multimodal choices for showing evidence for learning • Action research with embedded reflection tools
Assessment OF Learning	Reviewing and updating student portraits with end-of-unit data Reviewing unit goals in relation to desired outcomes Considering the correspondence among standards, instruction, and assessment	Utilized by administrators and school leaders and teachers with input from students • Student score reports from annual and interim tests communicated to families and caregivers in multiple languages • Information in student portraits • Grade-level, school, and district rubrics (e.g., from common assessment) • School or district student portfolios with selected entries

Let's take a trip to Uniondale, New York, where Victoria Lore, a high school English teacher, speaks to the coordination of the three assessment approaches—AS, FOR, and OF learning—in her integrated class and their overall impact on teaching and learning.

- *Assessment AS Learning: Multilingual learners engage in peer discussions and self-reflection, identifying areas of strength and growth in both content and language.*
- *Assessment FOR Learning: My coteacher and I use this approach to adjust ongoing instruction. For instance, if assessment reveals that students are struggling with a specific language concept or content area skill, we both provide additional targeted support to enhance [the] students' academic and language potential.*
- *Assessment OF Learning: Whether collaboratively designed by my coteacher and me or agreed upon by the grade-level team, summative assessment provides a comprehensive picture of our multilingual learners' progress and overall achievement. This assessment approach helps us make informed decisions about our next steps for supporting our students.*

Integrating these assessments creates a dynamic and supportive learning environment for multilingual students, promoting not only academic growth but also fostering self-awareness and engagement in the learning process within my classroom.

In our earlier work, we advocated for the following: "Linguistically and culturally sustainable classroom assessment, where teachers and students co-plan and co-construct performance tasks, use mutually agreed upon criteria for success, and provide evidence *FOR* and *AS* learning, represents equitable practices for multilingual learners."

—Margo Gottlieb and Andrea Honigsfeld (2020, p. 135)

You may not be acquainted with assessment AS, FOR, and OF learning; if so, what are some of your initial thoughts? How might you coordinate these approaches within the instructional and assessment cycles? How might you collaborate with colleagues and students in enacting these approaches?

What Should We Do Before Leaving This Stop?

Reflect on Our Successes!

In this chapter, we present a unique combination of two cycles you might be familiar with—or not—the collaborative instructional cycle and the assessment cycle. We explored how they work in tandem and why it is essential to align the phases of assessment with the components of the collaboration cycle.

Collaborative instructional and assessment practices are dynamic, fluid, and cyclical—each time new evidence for student learning is collected, you can reevaluate your students' progress. Coassessment and shared reflection time can also help determine next steps with your students. As you move around the assessment cycle, here are some questions to ask:

- How are your students going to contribute to the assessment cycle?
- How are you going to collect evidence for student learning?
- How are you going to ensure that the data represent a balance among assessment AS, FOR, and OF learning?
- How are you going to makes sense of the information you gather?
- How are you going to share the information with students and their families?
- What actions are you going to take based on the information?

When you engage in (a) intentionally gathering evidence for student learning, (b) jointly examining students' academic, social-emotional, language and literacy development, and (c) making shared decisions about what next steps may best advance student learning, you come to see how assessment informs instruction and is a collaborative endeavor benefitting all.

Where Do We Go Next?

Heading Toward Our Destination!

The tri-part system of collaborative assessment AS, FOR, and OF learning ensures a multidimensional approach not only to assessment practices but also to collaborative planning and instruction. When you and your colleagues systematically examine what your students can do and plan accordingly, you are creating a more equitable learning environment for everyone. In the next three chapters, we will take a closer look at these three approaches to assessment through the lens of collaboration.

We start with assessment AS learning in Chapter 3, centering multilingual learners as we guide them in developing agency over their own learning. We have seen many teachers conscious of or focused on assessment FOR learning in their classrooms as they interact with students, the topic of Chapter 4. School and district leaders along with teachers might find assessment OF learning to be the most concrete since it is directly connected to standards-based goals and outcomes. We always keep in mind in our travels that across all three approaches, we apply principles of linguistic and cultural sustainability as the guiding light for our journey.

Our sequence of assessment AS, FOR, and OF learning illustrates how relationships among students, students and teachers, and teachers and school leaders can help drive more equitable decisions in classrooms and schools. We realize that this trio of approaches represents one perspective and way of looking at assessment—one that empowers, builds agency, and encourages autonomy for multilingual learners (Gottlieb, 2024). Our goal with this book is to offer you a road map where we position multilingual learners as capable, deliberate, and self-reflective—across all phases and approaches of assessment—as educators facilitate the journey of student learning.

Collaborative Assessment AS Learning 3

Assessment is the engine which drives student learning.

—John Cowan

Where Are We Going?

Multilingual Learners Will Tell Us!

It's the start of the new school year, and there continues to be a growing presence of multilingual learners throughout the Katherine Johnson campus. The third-grade teacher team is brainstorming activities for students to become acquainted with each other and begin to form a community of learners. The teachers want to establish comradery and trust within warm, inviting, and safe classrooms. Once established, the ultimate destination for the students is to become confident and independent learners through their participation in day-to-day experiences as they engage in assessment AS learning.

One of the teacher team's goals for the year is to increase student–student interaction to foster their oral language development within a multiliteracies framework. A strategy the teachers routinely embed in instruction and assessment is dialogic communication. In this chapter, you will see multilingual learners converse with each other in prompted dialog as they integrate content and language, seek alternatives for plausible responses, come to consensus, and take turns speaking and listening. All the while, the students control the discourse as their exchange flows quite naturally while the teacher observes their interaction without inserting herself in the conversation.

Finding Our Way

Let's visit a third-grade math class to see student interaction in action. As a means of reviewing concepts on quantity involving addition and subtraction, students are invited with their partners to generate "How many" and "how many more" questions that involve the hundreds place. The dialog that follows revolves around two students making sense of mathematical problem solving through shared thinking. The partners explain to each other how they might obtain their answers. Later the students represent and interpret their data by graphing the information, comparing the quantities, and presenting their findings to their peers.

But first, let's listen to the conversation between two students, Marisol and Daniel, during their initial exchange. Notice the natural flow as students seamlessly integrate math content with the language for math. You may also note Marisol's interplay between Spanish and English, her natural use of translanguaging, which helps deepen understanding of her language use and, in this instance, gain metalinguistic awareness.

A MATH CONVERSATION BETWEEN TWO THIRD GRADERS

Marisol: Pues, we need to figure out "How many?" and why. ¿Qué hacemos? How about "How many days of school?" We can divide that by months or weeks. What else?

Daniel: Maybe "How many students in our school?"

Marisol: What about "How many students in second and third grades?"

Daniel: I like that question. Or maybe "How many more second graders than third graders?" What should we do?

Marisol: Well, there are four classes of second grade and three classes of third grade. We need to find out el total—how many students in all. How can we do that?

Daniel: We can go to each room and count the students.

Marisol: Or we can ask the teachers how many students. Or go to the office to find out.

Daniel: Then we add up the numbers in each class to get the sum.

Marisol: That's not "some," it's everyone!

Daniel: No, sum means "all together."

Marisol: How do you know?

Daniel: Because "suma" in Spanish and "sum" in English mean the same thing—to add to get the "total," another word that is the same in both languages.

Marisol: ¡Qué chévere!

Student–student collaboration, as illustrated in the give and take of the dialog, is the centerpiece of coassessment AS learning. In our journey, we will witness how students working together gradually take on responsibility and ownership to become drivers of their own learning. Since students are active participants in the process, they help set the destination, choose pathways to showcase their learning, and strategically engage in student self- and peer assessment along the way.

How do we get there? We will show you how to nurture multilingual learners' self-awareness and growth, their language, their conceptual and social-emotional development, and note the students' ongoing progress in knowing, reasoning, and communicating. Simultaneously, you most likely will observe multilingual learners establishing rapport with their peers.

Collaborative assessment AS learning is built on relationships between and among students and secondarily, between teachers and students within a safeguarded community of learners, the classroom. As illustrated in Figure 3.1, we invite you to envision this approach of collaborative assessment as a continuum of ownership of learning (from A to C). In shifting the locus of control from teachers to students during instruction and assessment activities, ultimately, students increasingly become the arbiters of their own learning. Being embedded in instruction and indistinguishable from it, assessment AS learning stimulates student thought while contributing to their trust-building and self-regulation.

Figure 3.1 Shifting the Locus of Control in Collaborative Assessment AS Learning to Students

(A) Teacher guided — (B) Teacher facilitated — (C) Student initiated

These moves within assessment AS learning exemplify a gradual release of responsibility where students progressively gain confidence and self-sufficiency. Think about your own classroom. Although there is not a timetable in moving along the continuum, you should be aware of where you are positioned with student-focused embedded assessment and where you wish to go with your students.

> The gradual release of responsibility model has a long-standing and sound foundation on established socio-cognitive principles and instructional theories such as those espoused by Jerome Bruner, Lev Vygotsky, and Anne Brown. David Pearson and Margaret Gallagher, the developers of the framework in 1983, recognized a need for teachers to be responsible for leading and scaffolding instruction, even as they supported learners in moving toward independent application of strategies and independence.
>
> —P. David Pearson et al. (2019, p. 2)

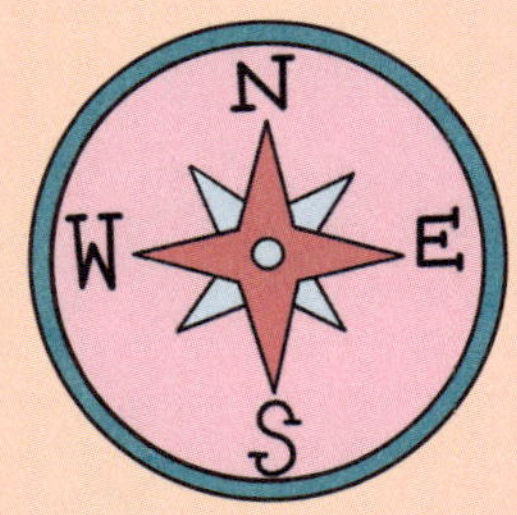

We introduce assessment AS learning as a teacher-guided activity (A on the continuum), a collaborative endeavor where initially you model an activity, strategy, or skill within a content area and then guide your students to interact with classmates. In turn, students practice with each other based on agreed-upon norms while giving and receiving feedback from peers or teachers. Ultimately, students work on their own and, at times, check with others to determine the extent to which they have met their expectations.

Considering Our Strategic Options

Many student-centered classroom strategies are associated with assessment AS learning, so there is always another route to take if one proves too challenging.

Think-pair-share and its variations, for instance, is a widespread teaching strategy where you generally offer a prompt or open question to spark student interaction and collaboration. Here's an example in which groups of four students engage in self-assessment based on a familiar content-based activity.

AN EXAMPLE STUDENT THINK-PAIR-SHARE-SQUARE REFLECTIVE ACTIVITY

Keeping their learning target in mind, during a lesson,

- Student 1 thinks of an open-ended wh-question (in which there is not a single correct answer) related to the topic or issue at hand (or chooses one from teacher suggestions).
- Students 2 and 3 generate different responses to the question.
- Student 4 selects one of the two responses and justifies the choice with two to three reasons.
- Students 1, 2, and/or 3 challenge the response chosen by Student 4 with their own pieces of evidence.
- Students 1, 2, 3, and 4 then decide on a final collective response, defend how they have met their learning target, and offer the strongest evidence for making their claim.

Midway along the continuum of assessment AS learning (approaching B in Figure 3.1), we see the teacher's role move to one of facilitator. Here you might cultivate a shared responsibility for learning by extending students access to linguistic and cultural resources (e.g., digital apps and materials in multiple languages) during assessment, introduced during instruction (even though you may or may not be well versed in your students' languages). Given an agreed-upon project, for example, you and your students might brainstorm a list of viable routes for meeting their goal. Students then select their path from an array of multimodal options (e.g., visual, audio, graphic, kinesthetic, linguistic) to show evidence for their learning.

A coteaching model is ideal for initiating assessment AS learning as there are two teachers to model collaboration of student learning. In Westbury, New York, Shanel Barrett, a third-grade classroom teacher in an Integrated Coteaching (ICT) class, and her coteacher engage in assessment AS learning by facilitating reflective practices, like personalized goal setting, that foster a strong sense of student agency. They find that this assessment approach transforms multilingual learners into active participants in their learning journey.

"The concept of student agency is rooted in the principle that students have the ability and the will to positively influence their own lives and the world around them."

—OECD (2019, p. 1)

Ultimately, in assessment AS learning, your students become mediators of their own learning, proceeding toward C on the continuum (last move in Figure 3.1). Here students generate themes or topics to explore, coconstruct criteria for success with classmates, and together, with your endorsement, set the parameters for engaged learning. Students are encouraged to pursue their own interests by drawing from their lived experiences inside and out of school. As a result, student-driven assessment empowers the students to explore their own ideas, whether it's younger students' engaged in invented play or older students' participation in service learning. Here's a short classroom vignette from Johnson elementary school that illustrates a student-initiated assessment project.

Let's Protect Our Friends!

A vivid example of assessment AS learning comes directly from third graders from Johnson elementary who have witnessed an increased number of car and bike incidents by their school and present this burning issue at their class meeting. After weighing the pros and cons of various options, the class takes the initiative to design a new sign to display around the community. The project is designed for the students to pursue their individual interests with a common set of descriptors to evaluate their end products.

Each student first chooses among three options:

1. Create a set of multilingual logos for the sign based on community exploration.
2. Configure the dimensions, shapes, sizes, and fonts of the signs.
3. Use Google Maps to investigate various street signs around the community.

An expert student from each option then forms a three-person team to craft each group's sign. Ultimately the class plans to act on this real-world issue by bringing their signs, along with video evidence from interviews with families and classmates, to argue its case at a town council meeting.

How Will We Get There?

Multilingual Learners Will Lead the Way!

At this stop in our journey, we invite you to accentuate your students' critical and growing role in collaborating and contributing to classroom assessment and, in doing so, becoming coassessors and owners of their learning. We shall witness how student-engaged assessment AS learning flips the traditional role of evaluating and ranking students to one that is stimulating, motivating, and personally engaging (Berger et al., 2014). Let's explore how multilingual learners, along with their peers, in traveling the highways and byways of assessment AS learning:

- Connect to assessment-embedded curriculum through their individual passions and collective lived experiences
- Actively participate in codesigning classroom assessment activities and tasks
- Carve and select their own pathways to reach their learning targets and goals that lead to and exemplify criteria for success
- Analyze information throughout the assessment cycle and engage in self-reflection
- Offer constructive feedback to each other to move their learning forward
- Develop self-identities, self-regulation, and autonomy as learners

Let's turn now to a high school example of assessment AS learning. During a unit of study on social justice and equity, Andrea Dell'Olio's and Bridget McElroy's students at the High School for Health Professions & Human Services in New York City generated a list of possible essay questions, thus coconstructing the end-of-unit assessment task while expressing their own interests. They then prioritized those themes that were most meaningful to them before launching into their research.

The following are some questions the high school students wished to pursue:

- *Why do people in power feel the need to oppress others?*
- *Why do some people find it difficult to trust someone in authority in society?*
- *How do people of power affect minorities/people of color's actions and thoughts?*
- *How do individuals who are part of two different worlds find a healthy way to balance them?*
- *How does a person's environment influence the decisions they make?*
- *Is protesting or rioting a way to bring about real change in societal problems?*

Note: Andrea Dell'Olio would like to honor her many years of collaboration with Bridget McElroy, who passed away prior to the publication of this book.

"The rigorous process of learning to develop and ask questions offers students the invaluable opportunity to become independent thinkers and self-directed learners."

—Dan Rothstein and Luz Santana (2011, p. 3)

Another real-life example comes from a middle school math class in New York, where Catherine Rainis Bura's students participate in reflective practices integral to assessment AS learning. This is what Catherine shared with us about her work:

> *In my class, students track their mathematical progress in their understanding of concepts and problem solving skills. This introspective process helps students deepen their ownership of the learning experience. Given math problems during a unit, the students evaluate their work and color code their progress in red, yellow, or blue to see first-hand how they grow throughout the unit. This proactive approach not only enhances the students' mathematical skills but also instills a sense of agency and responsibility, empowering students to actively steer their learning path in mathematics.*

Why Is Collaborative Assessment AS Learning Important in Our Journey?

It Honors Multilingual Learners' Voices and Choices!

For multilingual learners, collaborative assessment is a social practice where students are active participants. In it, you and your coteachers help pave the pathways to student success by offering encouragement, support, direction, and resources along with a safe welcoming space for them to thrive. Collaborative assessment AS learning centers students and elevates their status within the power structure of a classroom.

Educator Promises for Collaborative Assessment AS Learning

For multilingual learners and other minoritized students, we suggest that you coconstruct a set of promises to account for the primacy of student ownership in the learning process. In assessment AS learning, you will notice that in each statement, "students" lead the way. Here is a sample set of teacher-generated promises for assessment AS learning adopted by the Katherine Johnson campus.

As a teacher, I promise that:

- Students are honored and nurtured as individuals or as team members to reach their full potential.
- Students' linguistic and cultural assets, grounded in their home and community life, serve as the foundation for further learning and interaction with others.
- Student characteristics and histories are infused into curriculum, instruction, and assessment.

- Students can depend on and trust each other as they engage in instruction and assessment.
- Students' multiple cultural and experiential perspectives contribute to the health and vitality of classroom instruction and assessment.
- Student voice makes a difference in shaping how multilingual learners approach learning and show evidence for learning.
- Student choice is respected by peers and teachers as part of their social and emotional development.
- Students' contexts for interaction and access to linguistically and culturally relevant resources factor into instruction and assessment.
- Students' evidence for learning is always interpreted through a multilingual multicultural lens.
- Students participate in paired, small group, and classroom decision-making to learn and assess their learning from one another.

Notice how "students," the focus of assessment AS learning, are the watchword for these promises. You and your team might consider converting these promises into a checklist or a rating scale for your school as you participate in collaborative conversations and action planning around how to position your students in assessment. You might also take these promises and convert them into an action plan to incorporate into a year-long professional learning venture.

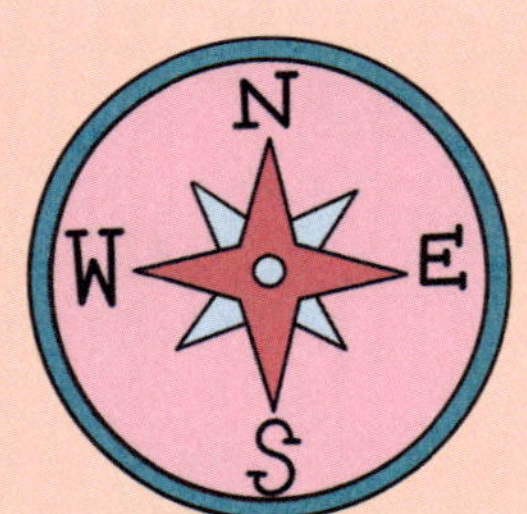

"If learning cannot be separated from the actions in which it is embodied, then assessment too must be situated. This implies that assessment is carried out alongside learning, not after learning."

—Mary E. James (2023, p. 15)

How Should We Prepare for Assessment AS Learning?

By Building Relationships!

An important theme of our journey that is reinforced in the promises of collaborative assessment is the formation and nurturing of valued relationships as the basis for student learning and development.

In our travels, we keep on running into a triad of collaborative assessment approaches. Assessment AS learning along with assessment FOR and OF learning creates a robust model (Gottlieb, 2016, 2021, 2024). We have chosen this model to represent the shift in the locus of control in classrooms from teachers to students and to instill agency along the way for both. Illustrated in Figure 3.2, collaborative assessment AS, FOR, and OF learning for multilingual learners is

- Focused on making and maintaining personal connections
- Geared around formulating agreed-upon learning targets and accompanying evidence
- Interwoven in collaborative instructional and assessment cycles
- Seamlessly integrated into classroom activities and tasks
- Multifaceted, involving multiple users, languages, and modalities
- Balanced in its representation of evidence

Figure 3.2 The Centrality of Multilingual Learners in Collaborative Assessment AS, FOR, and OF Learning

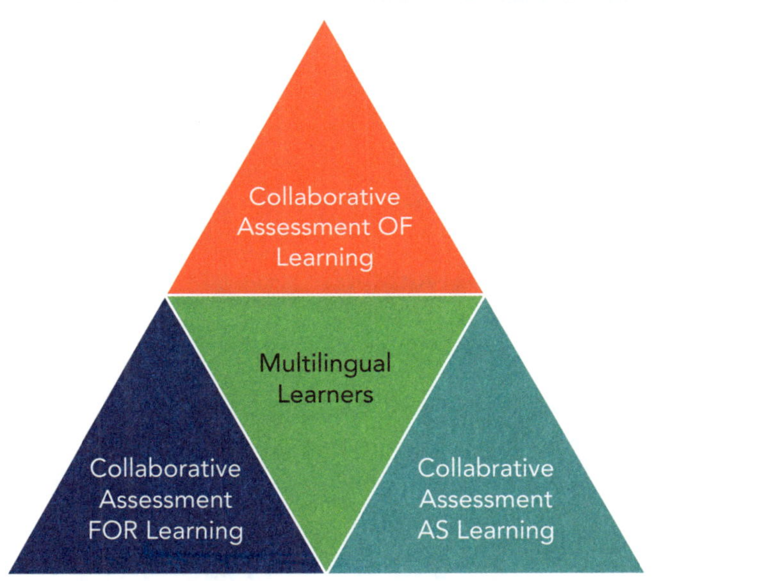

What do you notice about this assessment model that distinguishes it from others you may be familiar with? What comes to mind when you hear the words "collaborative" and "learning" attached to assessment? In essence, how does this model humanize what typically is associated with assessment?

While Chapters 4 and 5 elaborate on collaborative assessment FOR and OF learning, we choose to introduce the model here so that you can envision the expanding roles and responsibilities of multilingual learners in the process. It is the formation of trusting relationships and the blending of these assessment approaches that we emphasize throughout our journey. At this stop, however, we highlight the growing bond and interdependence among students as they engage in collaborative assessment AS learning.

To solidify the presence of multilingual learners in assessment AS learning, we return to the five phases of the collaborative assessment cycle. Figure 3.3 invites you to discuss with colleagues ways to elevate the status of student engagement in the assessment process. To complete the chart, generate ideas of how multilingual learners might add their voice to each phase.

Figure 3.3 The Role of Students in Each Phase of the Collaborative Assessment Cycle

PHASE OF THE ASSESSMENT CYCLE	HOW CAN STUDENTS CONTRIBUTE?
1. Planning (co)assessment	
2. Collecting and organizing assessment information	
3. Interpreting assessment information and providing feedback	
4. Evaluating and reporting assessment information	
5. Taking action based on assessment results	

Perhaps you are not convinced yet of the value of assessment AS learning. That said, we realize there is always some opposition to the road we take, thus we introduce a warning sign to alert you to what might be some obstruction or detour ahead.

What Are Some Caveats/Challenges Along the Way?

Cautionary Steps

Assessment AS Learning Is Distinct From Formative Assessment

We realize that many of you classify assessment purposes as either "formative" or "summative." However, "formative," the purpose most associated with everyday classroom assessment practices, has taken on an array of meanings. Popham (2011), for example, applies formative assessment practices to five situations that revolve around teachers making a(n)

- Immediate instructional adjustment
- Near-future instructional adjustment
- Last-chance instructional adjustment
- Learning tactic adjustment
- Classroom climate shift (p. 14)

Given these situations, you might ask, "Where are the students, and do they have any say in these instructional decisions?" As you have probably noticed, we prefer the term assessment AS learning to accentuate students at the core of the cycle and overseers of actions taken. We believe it is more descriptive of the positioning of *learning* within the assessment experience for multilingual learners and their relationships with peers as members of a community of practice.

"Categorizing types of tasks as formative or summative is a harmful misuse of these terms. Formative and summative are terms we use to describe *how we use* the information from assessment. . . . We have a formative period of time and summative points in time."

—Lee Ann Jung (2023, p. 159)

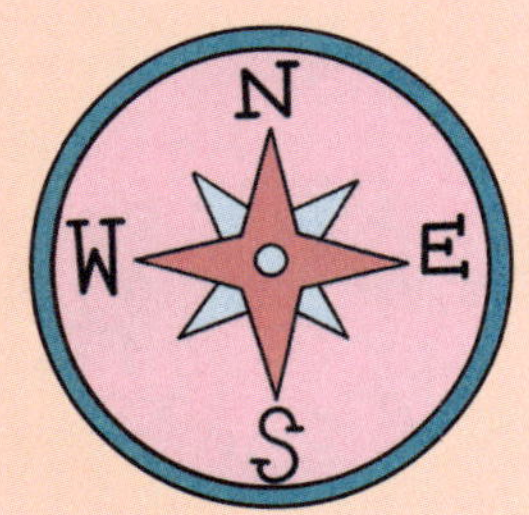

What do formative assessment practices mean to you? To your colleagues? To your school leaders? It might prove interesting for you and your colleagues to explore your curricular materials and literature for different applications of the term. Then modify the definitions you encounter to make them more student centric. In converting the term "formative assessment" to assessment AS learning, you have just become more inclusive of your students!

It May Take Time to Change Your Assessment Mindset

No matter where you travel, inevitably there are some bumps in the road. You need to remember that introducing and sustaining assessment AS learning is student driven and, depending on your students, may take longer than anticipated. Remember, every student is an individual with a unique history, personality, and identities.

There are several factors that might contribute to the varying lengths of time necessary for instilling the promises for assessment AS learning in your classroom. You may not be aware of the variability among your multilingual learners; student portraits may shed some light on their unique qualities. In addition, considering the cluster of characteristics that defines each student, think of whether the student has

- Strong or weak relationships with family members; in some cases, for example, primary family members may be absent
- Witnessed or endured trauma and hardship
- Had interrupted schooling due to mobility or chronic absenteeism
- Recently arrived and is becoming acclimated to U.S. schools and customs
- Varying degrees of literacy in multiple languages
- Been assigned different numerical categories (e.g., language proficiency or tier of multi-tiered system of supports) rather than descriptors of what they can do

What Do We Need to Pack?

An Array of Activities!

As we embark on the journey for assessment AS learning, we'll pack a suitcase full of strategies and activities to foster student collaboration and personal reflection. In addition, we must pack items to ensure that the students have access to varied resources to optimize their opportunities to learn. After all, our suitcase must be appropriate for all the situations we might encounter in our travels.

Coteaching and coassessing give multilingual learners space and time to grow. As teachers, you have come to recognize that this is a personalized process that depends on the age of the student, their home life, social-emotional development, and school experiences. As you think about what instructional and assessment items for your students to place in their suitcases, you should consider the following:

- Goals and criteria for learning
  - Coconstructing learning targets and goals
  - Creating and applying criteria for success to student work samples
  - Defending interpretation of the criteria with evidence for learning
- Original student work
  - Having students engage in self- and peer assessment, such as writing pieces, oral language samples, or visual displays based on preset criteria
  - Guiding students in revising drafts based on self, peer, and teacher feedback
- Final products
  - Applying criteria for learning (e.g., rubrics or descriptors) to interpret final products
  - Practicing oral presentations, coconstructing models, or putting together displays for peers, teachers, family members, or the community

(Adapted from Gottlieb & Honigsfeld, 2020)

Peer Evaluation Tools

Another effective strategy for assessment AS learning was shared with us by Alycia Owen, a secondary ELD/EAL coach, who created a novel and fun way to organize peer editing sessions:

- *Teacher distributes completed essays so that students do not have their own papers.*

- *The peer editor uses a scavenger hunt format to look for important elements in the essay and marks a check upon completion (see Figure 3.4).*
- *Peer editors return scavenger hunt checklist and original essay to its author for review.*
- *Students review peer feedback independently. Time is given for students to meet with their peer reviewer to ask any clarifying questions and to give positive feedback.*

Figure 3.4 A Peer Editing Scavenger Hunt

✓	SCAVENGER HUNT!
	Find the writer's **claim**. Circle it.
	Find places in the text where **reasons** are offered to support the claim. Underline them.
	Find **evidence** offered by the writer to support the claim. Highlight these areas of the text.
	Find the sentence(s) that include(s) the **counterclaim**. Draw a star on top of the sentence(s).
	Find **transition words and phrases**. Draw a box around each one you find.

When we unpack our suitcase, we must be ready for all occasions, a heterogeneous mix of students, and often, if we are language specialists or coaches, a range of grade levels. Let's return to the scenario between the two third graders at the beginning of the chapter and think of how we might capture student evidence AS learning. Here we observe a conversation between a bilingual student pair that exemplify dialogic teaching with learners coconstructing shared knowledge, critiquing their own ideas, and ultimately having control over the content and decision-making (Mercer, 2003).

Dialogic Talk Between Students

As a dialogic teacher, you see your multilingual learners as partners in the learning process rather than passive recipients of knowledge (Swaffield, 2011). In doing so, students take control of the situation and dialogic teaching becomes part of collaborative assessment AS learning.

As your students interact with each other, you might wish to analyze what multilingual learners say and take note of progress in their oral language development. Figure 3.5 is a sample checklist for teacher and/or student use during dialogic talk throughout a school year. You may wish to elaborate, expanding the "Yes, we do!" column, and jot down the student(s), date, and specific instances of language use.

Figure 3.5 Assessing Multilingual Learners During Dialogic Talk: An Observation Tool

WHEN WATCHING MULTILINGUAL LEARNERS AND OTHER STUDENTS TALK TO EACH OTHER, WE HEAR OR SEE	YES, WE DO!
1. Questions that reinforce and extend student thinking	
2. Details being added in the students' preferred language(s)	
3. Respectful challenges to what peers say (with reasons or evidence)	
4. Reasoning and justification of students' ideas	
5. Negotiation and validation of students' stance	
6. Acceptance when students change their minds, speak with hesitation, or use imperfect language	
7. Students feeling safe in sharing their perspectives or opinions	
8. Gestures or other multimodal means that communicate or reinforce ideas	
9. Thoughtful responses and student consideration for one another	
10. Cooperation and collaboration in students agreeing on an action to take	
Noticings as students interact:	

Classroom talk and questioning are strategic ways for you to elicit evidence of student understanding and misunderstandings during assessment AS learning that inform next instructional steps. In fact, these strategies are in themselves powerful student-centered learning activities. When your students engage in listening and contribute to the flow of targeted content-related conversation, they cocreate and expand their knowledge base and comprehension. Additionally, dialog coupled with peer assessment helps your students learn within authentic contexts as they negotiate with others (Swaffield, 2011).

Participation in thoughtful and reasoned dialog prompts your students to use language as a tool for both independent and collective thinking. In collaborative assessment AS learning, conversational partners practice using language for multiple purposes: to reason, reflect, inquire, and clarify their thinking with others. According to Jeff Zwiers (2019), who has conducted extensive classroom research on academic conversations, "Every conversation, in fact, should build at least one idea, and participants should walk away a little different—with more knowledge, a changed perspective, more conviction, or a new way to solve a problem" (p. 5).

Discussion Boards

Student interaction can be prompted with a range of activities. These strategies maximize student engagement while providing teachers with valuable information on multilingual learners' oral language development. Here are some strategies for your classroom to keep students active and excited about learning:

- *Back-to-back and face-to-face*: First students produce challenging open-ended questions on topics that are approved by peers and their teacher. Then, taking turns, they read their questions while standing back-to-back with a peer. Given think time of a minute or two, multilingual learners in general, and those in bilingual and dual-language classrooms in particular, are encouraged to use their multiple languages. Once you or a student signals face-to-face, the students turn around and share their responses. Questioning can continue with the same partner or switch to a new one.
- *Carousel brainstorm*: In pairs or threesomes, students rotate the room brainstorming a joint response to open-ended questions that have been displayed on individual posters. Each group has a different colored marker and has devised an acronym as a team name.
- *Gallery walk*: Using the information posted during the carousel brainstorm, students can then take sticky notes to give feedback and sign them with their team name as they travel clockwise around the room. After completing the round, then you can go from station to station with additional feedback and follow-up questions.

Coupling Oral Language With Literacy for Multilingual Learners

We have to be careful in our travels not to forget our must-have items for our suitcase. As noted in research reports and policy briefs, multilingual learners' oral language development is a necessary component of their overall literacy, yet it is often overlooked in a literacy block. We have seen how dialogic talk and discussion boards prompt student–student interaction using multilingual learners' full linguistic resources, yet this strategy alone is not enough for multilingual learners to attain grade-level literacy.

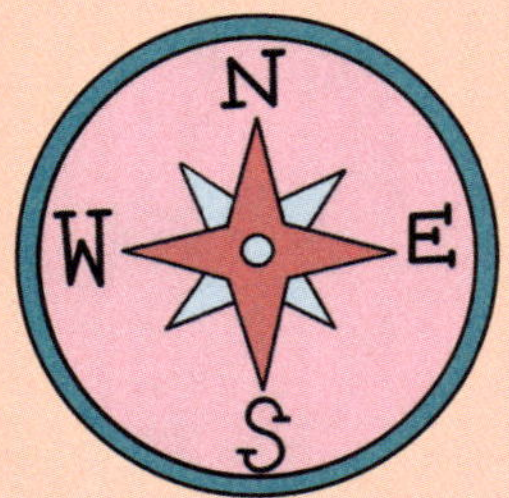

Major research reports and policy briefs on K–12 literacy over the last decades accentuate two critical components for multilingual learners: (a) a necessary added dimension of oracy (oral language development) and (b) the advantage of accessing students' "home" language for (bi)literacy development.

—Diane August and Timothy Shanahan, 2006; Margo Gottlieb, 2023b; National Academies of Sciences, Engineering, and Medicine (NASEM), 2017; National Academy of Education, 2020; National Committee for Effective Literacy (NCEL), 2022

You should devote some time as a schoolwide community of practice, grade-level team, or cross-disciplinary team to investigate these and other literacy reports and their specific stance for multilingual learners. You might consider using the template that follows to help formulate grade-level or schoolwide collaborative assessment policies.

Comparing Findings From Literacy-Related Research Reports and Briefs That Pertain to Multilingual Learners: Implications for Collaborative Assessment

Name of Report and Authors (if applicable)	Year of Publication and Reference	Major Findings/ Evidence/ Guidance	Confirmatory or Counter Evidence From Personal Practice	Suggested Collaborative Assessment Policy for Multilingual Learners Based on Multiple Sources of Evidence
1.				
2.				

Take a critical stance:

- What does the research say and not say?
- How does the research align to your practice?
- Why does it matter to teachers of multilingual learners?

Teacher or school leadership teams might jigsaw the different research positions or reports and then compare their findings as the basis for formulating or revisiting school or district policy.

An analysis of these reports should yield insight into the treatment of multilingual learners in literacy research and raise additional questions for you to explore. For example, should multilingual learners' literacies in multiple languages be tapped as part of their English literacy development? As a follow-up, you might consider, if you haven't already, designing action research of your own around the value of coinstructing and coassessing multilingual learners' (bi)literacy development.

Multiliteracies for Multilingual Learners

You may or may not be familiar with the term "mulitliteracies," but over the last two decades, it has gained prominence in educational circles. Introduced by the New London Group in 1996, multiliteracies goes beyond structured literacy or the science of reading, and for some multilingual learners, even biliteracy (Gottlieb, 2023b). Multiliteracies is a concept that highlights the presence of and reliance on multiple modes of communication; it entails understanding, creating, and interpreting meaning as students pursue varied pathways to learning. Today, the explosion of digital tools, such as generative artificial intelligence (AI), is a stunning example of the expanding role of student collaboration in classroom settings around technology, one that exemplifies multiliteracies that we cannot ignore (Kim et al., 2022).

With multiliteracies, we legitimatize multimodal and multilingual perspectives within instruction and assessment as it is a means for multilingual learners to use their linguistic and cultural resources to better understand content. Multilingual learners' use of multiliteracies is personal as it involves their development of metacognitive (consciously reflecting on one's thinking), metalinguistic (consciously reflecting on one's use of and comparison between languages), and metacultural (consciously reflecting on one's sociocultural identity in learning and seeing the world) awareness (Gottlieb, 2024). Let's see how these three facets of multiliteracies represent assessment AS learning.

Metacognitive, Metalinguistic, and Metacultural Awareness

As we pack our bags, we begin to understand that there are two global phenomena that constitute and drive multiliteracies: (1) the growing presence of multilingual learners and (2) the increasing global impact of technology. If we dig deeper into our suitcase, we discover how multiliteracies not only enhances multilingual learners' technological expertise, but it also heightens students' metalinguistic, metacultural, and metacognitive awareness (Gottlieb, 2021; 2023a). As shown in Figure 3.6, we reveal multilingual learners' engagement in assessment AS learning by formulating questions that pertain to their growing awareness of language, culture, and thinking.

Figure 3.6 Fostering Metalinguistic, Metacultural, and Metacognitive Awareness Through Student Self-Assessment

GROWING AWARENESS IN MULTILINGUAL LEARNERS	QUESTIONS TO PROMOTE STUDENT SELF-REFLECTION
Metalinguistic awareness	• How do I compare different aspects of my languages to better understand both? • How do I use what I know in one language to predict what it might mean in another?
Metacultural awareness	• How do I move in and out of different cultures throughout the day? • How does living in multiple cultures help me be more caring or considerate?
Metacognitive awareness	• What do I already know about this topic or concept, and how can I apply it to new situations? • What strategies do I use to be more mindful of what I am thinking and why?

Alycia Owen, whom we met earlier in this chapter, collaborated with colleagues to develop several reflection prompts, many of which are used as entrance or exit tickets to stimulate multilingual learners' metacognitive and metalinguistic development. The prompts offer students time to be introspective and self-reflect on their place in the world as multilingual multicultural persons.

REFLECT

In our readings and discussions, we have identified many benefits of being multilingual. Which one is most important to you and why?

Imagine Your Future

It's 2030. Will it be apparent to the world that you are a polyglot? In what ways will being multilingual have shaped your life by then?

Words of Wisdom

As a person who understands and speaks multiple languages, what advice would you give to those who might be struggling to learn a new language?

Translanguaging

Describe a typical situation that demonstrates your use of translanguaging. When do you use your particular languages? How does translanguaging affect your ability to communicate?

Learning in English

How does knowing another language affect your ability to learn content-area subjects in English? Give an example or two.

A Note to My Teachers

Based on your experience learning academic English, what advice would you give your teachers?

Celebrating Success

Using only pictures and/or short phrases, create a graphic that celebrates your successes as a multilingual learner.

All students should have time to analyze their ways of thinking and articulate their thoughts, orally, in writing, or even in doodles. When they do so, they build their metacognitive, metalinguistic, and metacultural awareness. In Figure 3.7, we see students collaborate in assessment AS learning in thinking through the steps of their project.

Figure 3.7 Students Coassessing Their Metacognition in Partner or Group Work

An Example Rating Scale

Students should respond to the following statements to describe their thinking in planning, carrying out, and evaluating a project for a unit of learning (discussed more in depth in Chapter 5). Although presented as a rating scale, you should decide whether a checklist would be more appropriate for your students.

WHEN WORKING WITH MY GROUP OR MY PARTNER	NOT YET	SOMETIMES	MOST OF THE TIME	ALL THE TIME
We discuss what our learning target means.				
We talk to each other to help think through our project.				
We think about how to use content and language resources.				
We discuss our choices and decide how to present our evidence for learning.				
We choose how to show our thinking, such as with photos, diagrams, or graphics in addition to text.				
We think about the language we use when giving feedback on each other's project.				
We share thoughts with others on how our project met our learning goals.				

Adapted from Gottlieb (2024)

As we further inspect our suitcases, we realize that multiliteracies not only contributes to multilingual learners' identity formation and expand their awareness, but it also is apparent when students with shared languages engage in translanguaging, a natural occurrence between multilingual learners that entails the dynamic fluid interchange between shared languages.

Translanguaging

Multilingual learners bring all their language resources, including their translanguaging practices, along with them on their life journeys. We realize that in recent years, translanguaging has taken on many interpretations, however, idiolect, the language or speech patterns unique to an individual, is the one most associated with assessment AS learning. Despite this broad definition, when schools and districts assess general language proficiency (that is, assessment OF learning in English during standardized testing), translanguaging is either inhibited or prohibited (Otheguy et al., 2015). Therefore, classroom assessment must allow multilingual learners flexibility in showing content through students' customary language use.

Among multilingual learners, translanguaging also acts as a conversational tool (as illustrated in the dialog earlier in the chapter). In addition, it is a literacy-related instructional strategy present in text, including billboards, signs, literature, poetry, and song. Research on translanguaging in elementary school classrooms reveals it is "collaborative and agentive, socioculturally situated, culturally responsive, and a resource for as well as a process of learning" (Rajendram, 2019, p. iii).

At this collaborative assessment AS learning stop, you should take some time as a schoolwide community of practice, grade-level team, or cross-disciplinary team to investigate translanguaging as a strategy for multilingual learners to infuse in curriculum, instruction, and assessment. You do not have to be bilingual, nor do your students need to be in bilingual programs, to participate in the discussion. Once you come to consensus on your definition, discuss the extent to which translanguaging has had or can have a positive impact on multilinguals' learning.

Which Pathways Should We Take?

Ones That We Are Interested in Exploring!

There should always be multiple pathways for multilingual learners (and all students) to explore during learning and as options to show their learning (Soto et al., 2024). Equally important, we must realize that instruction is not a one-way street and that relationship building with students and colleagues is bidirectional. With a variety of roads to travel, collaborative assessment AS learning involves students leading the way. It is often easier said than done! Let's continue our sightseeing at this stop with some practical ways to yield the locus of control to our students.

We have mentioned how coassessment revolves around a partnership between teachers, perhaps a language specialist coupled with a content-area teacher, a teacher of multilingual learners and a coach, or a school's bilingual teachers,. When we speak of assessment AS learning, students are always the primary focus and communicators. As the relationship between you and your students moves along the pathway or continuum in Figure 3.1, your role becomes more unobtrusive. Here is when the act of *noticing* rather than *telling* becomes a central practice, where observation affects how you organize, represent, and interpret information (National Research Council, 2000).

Noticing

Teacher noticing is part of instruction and classroom assessment. It encompasses the processes through which you manage ongoing information as you attend to student relations, student learning, and student thinking (Sherin et al., 2011). And there is much information to manage! Figure 3.8 is an observational tool for you to help notice multilingual learners' use of language with their classmates in collaborative assessment AS learning during content-based language activities.

Figure 3.8 Gathering Information on Multilingual Learners' Language Use During Classroom Observation

COLLABORATIVE INSTRUCTIONAL ASSESSMENT ACTIVITY	EXAMPLE OF STUDENT'S LANGUAGE USE WITH PEERS (IN ENGLISH, ANOTHER LANGUAGE, OR BOTH)	STUDENT'S OVERALL EFFECTIVENESS IN COMMUNICATING (VERY, QUITE, SOMEWHAT)
Compare information from different sources		
Defend opinions or perspectives with evidence		
Summarize and reflect on experiences		
Re-enact historical or literary events		
Debate local issues		
Ask and answer questions (e.g., for information gathering)		

As teachers of multilingual learners, we must be vigilant as to *what* we focus on in our observations, *how* we reason based on our noticings, and *what* inferences we draw from the information. For example, if you look back on the use of translanguaging during the students' dialog, what do you notice? You might see it as a gesture of outreach and friendship, as well as the bonding between classmates. Additionally, in this instance, you might see how translanguaging serves to deepen mathematical learning through a student's insight into lexical (word-level) connections between Spanish and English (e.g., total, suma/sum) that show their metalinguistic awareness.

Noticing is an important attribute of teaching as teachers' perceptions of their students through an assets lens have implications for the social-emotional development of multilingual learners. The accumulation of teacher observations as students engage collaboratively in assessment AS learning sends a profound message regarding the intrinsic value of multilingual learners and the importance of their interactions (van Es, 2021). As we shall discover in our upcoming stop, assessment FOR learning, teacher and student feedback is also vital in collaborative classroom assessment to propel teaching and learning forward.

What Should We Do Before Leaving This Stop?

Reflect on Our Successes!

At our stop at assessment AS learning, we begin to shift from thinking of assessment as a means for measuring and recording student achievement to one that is an ongoing process or cycle to support student learning (Yin et al., 2022). We witness students becoming confident learners who are beginning to lead the way as they become positioned to be decision-makers. We encourage students to pause to self- and peer reflect to ascertain where they are in their learning and their goals for the future.

Careful to get to their destination following a GPS and other tracking devices, teachers notice the pathway each student takes in their social-emotional, language, and conceptual development. We have witnessed that when you empower your students through assessment AS learning,

- Students come to see themselves as lifelong learners
- Students and teachers become co-owners of learning
- Students are aware of how they are doing
- Students' strengths are accentuated
- Students actively engage in learning
- Students gain a sense of belonging

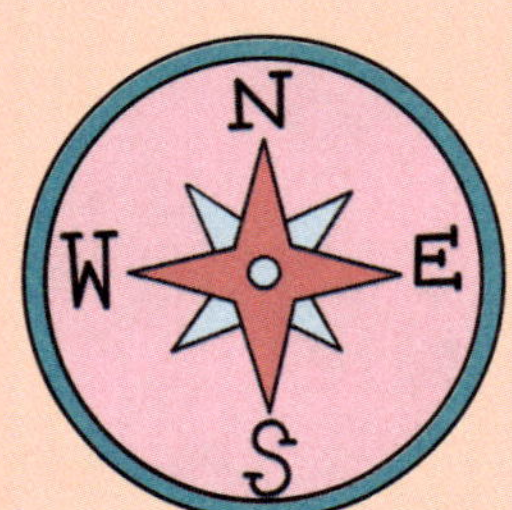

"When we shepherd students through curriculum without involving them—that is, when we act as learner managers instead of learner empowerers—we miss the opportunity to let them find their own way."

—Jacob Bruno (2021, para. 6)

Let's visit Holly Sawyer's classroom in Virginia, where her high school students regularly consult with their peers and give each other pointed feedback and support. In Figure 3.9, students are demonstrating assessment AS learning as they create Venn diagrams that compare and contrast a character's immigration story with their own.

Figure 3.9 A Collaborative Assessment AS Learning Activity

Where Do We Go Next?

Head Toward Our Destination!

We have seen in our assessment travels how multilingual learners interact with each other to deepen their thinking, develop positive interdependence, and become individually accountable—all components of collaborative learning (Lin, 2015). These interactive and collaborative actions in assessment AS learning foster student agency and are in contrast with classroom routines where teacher talk dominates, students speak one at a time, and inevitably, there is only one correct answer.

Ultimately, we believe that multilingual learners who work together in posing and solving problems, craft and accomplish shared goals through consensus building, engage in dialog, and offer evidence for learning are indeed practitioners of assessment AS learning. The longitudinal work of Proctor et al. (2021) reveals some helpful tenets of instruction that we have emphasized throughout this stop in our journey to date. To reiterate, as teachers of multilingual learners, you should:

- Highlight content-driven language as well as metalinguistic and metacultural awareness stemming from students' knowledge of the similarities and differences between languages and cultures
- Enact dialogic strategies to encourage students to engage in interaction and collaboration
- Coinstruct and coassess from a multilingual perspective that honors students' identities

As you look back on collaborative assessment AS learning with your students, here are some questions to ponder:

- How might you enhance teaching and learning in your classroom, teacher team, or school by centering your students?
- How might you create a warm and welcoming classroom culture where every student is valued and interaction between/among students is part of the classroom routine?
- How might you encourage multilingual learners to take the lead in classroom activities to advance their learning?
- How might you foster multilingual learners' identity formation through growing their metalinguistic, metacultural, and metacognitive awareness?
- What might you do to convince colleagues and administrators of the value of this assessment approach for all students?

In this chapter, we have seen individual multilingual learners gradually become molded into a caring and sharing classroom community. Through relationship building, we have witnessed how students gradually gain confidence, independence, and interdependence as they interact with each other during assessment-embedded instruction. At this stop, we have gained first-hand knowledge of how relationships are the onramp to learning (Hammond, 2015).

As students delve into collaborative assessment, we have honored their options that lead to their individual pathways of success. Equipped with agency, we ensure that our students' identities are valued—their means of learning, their languages and cultures, and their ways of being. Having explored collaborative assessment AS learning, we can't wait until we head toward our next stopover in our journey where students join with you, their teachers, in collaborative assessment FOR learning!

Collaborative Assessment FOR Learning

4

Our feedback is the oil which can lubricate this engine.

—Phil Race

Where Are We Going?

Wherever We Go, We're Going Together!

It's the end of October and the close of the first academic quarter on the Katherine Johnson campus. As a campuswide event, next week, students and teachers will send out personal invitations to families in their preferred language(s), devise a classroom agenda, and practice for the upcoming conference night for students and family members. Students have been keeping a collection of original pieces in their working portfolio, organized by their teachers; now it is time for students to claim ownership and cull its contents. Students are proud to show what they have accomplished to family members!

Each classroom has had a choice of storing individual student work, including photo journals and written texts, in a physical folder or cataloguing and archiving audio or video files and other multimedia tasks digitally. Teachers have reviewed entries with students on a regular basis, giving concrete timely feedback. Now it's the students' turn to review the comments one more time, revise their entries, and put the polishing touches on their favorite pieces.

Finding Our Way

As we have seen in assessment AS learning, coordination of classroom assessment efforts begins with students and highlights students throughout the process. At this stop in our journey, we feature collaborative assessment FOR learning and illustrate how this approach is geared to strengthening student–teacher relationships. This partnership exemplifies teamwork towards a common end—to elevate the status of classroom assessment to showcase students' accomplishments.

"The Handoff of learning represents the moment in the classroom when students are able to take ownership of their learning and become partners with their teachers and peers. It can only be achieved when teachers intentionally empower students."

—Mary Jane O'Connell and Kara L. Vandas (2015, p. 56)

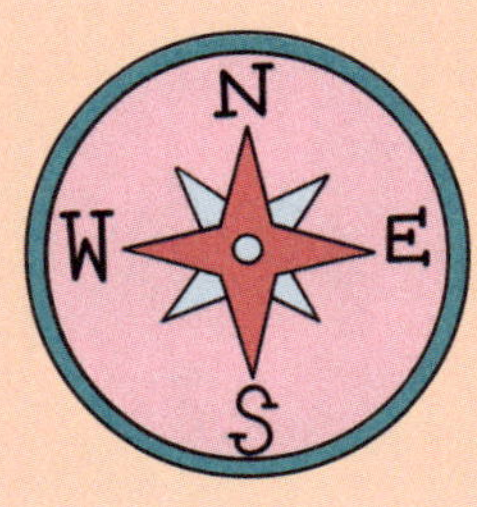

Let's peek into a fifth-grade classroom as everyone prepares for the upcoming *celebration of learning*. Multilingual learners are very excited to see the reaction of their families entering their classrooms that are filled with artifacts of students' multiple languages and cultures. Teachers have gotten to know and carefully nurture their students these first weeks of school. They are pleased with their multilingual learners' initial growth as well as their increasing independence.

In fact, from the beginning of the school year, one area in which teachers have mentored their fifth graders is in coconstructing integrated learning targets (see more on this topic on pages 81–82 of this chapter) to guide teaching and learning. Through ongoing professional learning, teachers have become aware of how integrating content and language is not only theoretically sound but also offers a unified and coordinated goal for learning for multilingual learners and their teachers (Gottlieb, 2022; Sherris, 2008; WIDA, 2020, 2023, among others).

Working together, content area teachers and language specialists have come to understand how examining connections between spoken and written discourse with intention results in multilingual learners' simultaneous development of content and language. This revelation has spurred coteachers to join forces in helping multilingual learners understand the role of language in content learning and the role of content in language learning.

Considering Our Options: Looking Into Technology

As part of its strategic plan, one of the annual goals on the Katherine Johnson campus is to meaningfully infuse technology in its many forms into curriculum, instruction, and assessment, thus accentuating multiliteracies for their multilingual learners. During classroom meetings, teachers and students have discussed the pros and cons of the increased role of technology in students' lives at home and at school. Students have shared their personal experiences in gaming, their interests in robotics, and their reliance on social media. The campus has created a comprehensive task force of families, students, teachers, support staff, and administrators to grapple with formulating an artificial intelligence (AI) policy.

Technology has proven to be a lynchpin for interaction and relationship building among students, families, and teachers, especially as part of assessment FOR learning. We must keep in mind, however, what Chandra et al. (2020) found: "Even in states with the smallest digital divides, one in four students still lacks adequate internet" (p. 3). In response to these and other contemporary challenges, the U.S. Department of Education, Office of Educational Technology (2023, 2024a) has published several guidelines to create an adequate and future-proof digital infrastructure. Among the most notable recommendations is the goal of achieving digital equity, which includes three essential components: availability, affordability, and adoption.

In most districts, there may be several different platforms and learning management systems. For example, in Johnson's K–5 division, Google Classroom allows teachers to post assignments, students to complete tasks independently or collaboratively, teachers to then provide feedback, and families to have input. Secondary classrooms are well supported with Canvas. Here digital portfolios or e-portfolios (such as Seesaw) can be used as powerful tools during student-led conferences (see Chapter 5).

One other unique way in which teachers have responded to students' interests through technology is by allocating space for classroom audio walls with QR codes and hyperlinked URLs of student audio or video recordings. Here teachers and students exchange notes based on specified descriptors, often using checklists to coordinate cross-checks as part of assessment. During reflection, students and teachers brainstorm and describe how different devices have been helpful in gaining conceptual and language understanding.

Technology, a vital aspect of multiliteracies, is becoming more and more prominent in instruction and assessment. How do you incorporate technology into your classroom routine? How are multilingual learners advantaged through technology? What specific tools do you find useful for multilingual learners and multilingual learners with exceptionalities in assessment FOR learning?

Extending Technology Into Assessment FOR Learning

Knowing that technology will forever be part of our students' lives, we should leverage their vested enthusiasm to embed into their learning experiences. For example, certain platforms allow you to engage in assessment FOR learning with students. Within instruction, you might choose a range of modalities to provide feedback to students, such as in-line comments (through video, audio, or text) and participation in online chats, email, or text. In this way, students can practice specific skills or key concepts (U.S. Department of Education, Office of Educational Technology, 2017).

"Technology can be a powerful tool for transforming learning. It can help affirm and advance relationships between educators and students, reinvent our approaches to learning and collaboration, shrink long-standing equity and accessibility gaps, and adapt learning experiences to meet the needs of all learners."

—U.S. Department of Education, Office of Educational Technology (2024b, para. 6)

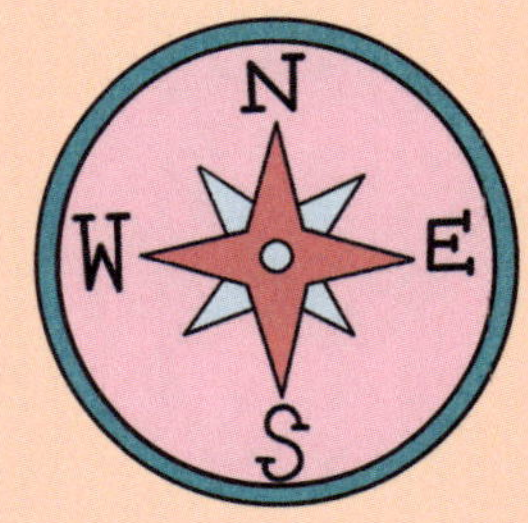

Through technology-embedded assessment, you can see how students are thinking during learning as you provide personalized feedback through classroom dashboards. Families can become more informed about student learning, especially if multilingual learners can communicate with family members in multiple languages. In turn, families' and multilingual learners' expertise can be tapped so that you better understand multilingual learners' contexts for instruction and assessment.

How Will We Get There?

Hand in Hand!

In this stop in our journey, we ask you to think about the unique characteristics of each student to optimize their learning opportunities and show what they know. The variability of multilingual learners, their family histories, lived experiences, preferences, languages, and cultures, blend together to form a classroom community of learners. Having a deep understanding of your students forms the basis for you to engage in assessment FOR learning with them.

There are many school-based configurations for forming collaborations (see Figure 4.1). Here are some of those possibilities for relationship building along with examples of their applicability to classroom assessment FOR learning. You and your colleagues may wish to insert names from your own setting to make the chart come to life as you think about forming partnerships around assessment practices.

Figure 4.1 Collaborative Assessment FOR Learning

RELATIONSHIP	ASSESSMENT FOR LEARNING EXAMPLE
Student–classroom teacher	Select pathways for engaging in learning and associated multimodal evidence
Student–classroom teacher and language specialist	Coconstruct integrated learning targets for content and language
Student–classroom teacher, language specialist, and special education teacher	Agree on the multimodalities that best represent the student's Individual Education Program as evidence for learning
Students–grade-level teacher team	Become familiar with oral and written feedback and how to respond using a positive tone
Students–dual language education team	Use multiple languages according to your language and assessment policy
Student–support team (e.g., social worker, speech pathologist, counselor)	Cocreate a plan, an agreement, or a contract with specific actions to achieve agreed-upon student-centered goals

Steps Along the Way

In assessment FOR learning, there are often specific demarcations in the road to help you navigate. Once you have selected a theme and/or essential question for a unit of learning, there are some strategic markers for you and your students to coplan to reach your destination. Four steps, indicated along the road that follows, can apply to a single lesson, a series of related lessons in a task, or a combination of tasks to form an entire unit of learning (Gottlieb, 2016).

Following the yellow-brick road . . .

Traveling along the four steps displayed in Figure 4.2, we see collaborative assessment FOR learning in action. Here students and teachers coplan the basics for classroom assessment for an individual or a series of lessons. While we recognize that you may use lesson "objectives," we prefer the term "learning targets" so you and your students have something specific to aim for. Later, in a parallel fashion in Figure 5.1, teachers interact with other educators following the steps for classroom assessment OF learning, outlining the parameters of a curricular unit.

Figure 4.2 Actions Associated With Collaborative Assessment FOR Learning at the Lesson Level

In classroom assessment FOR learning . . .

1. Students and teachers cocreate integrated learning targets (objectives)	• Combining content, language, and multimodalities • Representing students' languages, cultures, and experiences
2. Students and teachers coconstruct criteria for meeting the learning targets (objectives)	• Presenting information based on interactive activities • Converting standards to student-friendly statements
3. Students and teachers decide on evidence for meeting the learning targets (objectives)	• Offering multimodal supports • Giving examples or modeling
4. Students and teachers give and act on each other's feedback or reflect on learning	• Applying the criteria for success • Determining the extent to which integrated learning targets (objectives) have been met

To jumpstart lesson planning for each unit of learning, you might consider coplanning using the steps in assessment FOR learning as a template for you and your students. Given your theme and essential question, how might you systematically set up instruction with embedded assessment? Here are four questions to ask in designing lessons based on the template; how might you and your students respond?

A QUESTION FOR STEPS IN ASSESSMENT FOR LEARNING	HOW MIGHT YOU AND YOUR STUDENTS RESPOND?
1. What are our learning targets (objectives) for the lesson?	
2. How do we know we have reached our learning targets (what are our criteria)?	
3. In what ways do we show our learning (what is our evidence)?	
4. How does feedback from our teachers and peers help us reach our learning targets?	

Checking Out Assessment Within Curricular Frameworks

At the beginning of our journey, we illustrate the assessment cycle as a five-phase iterative process centered on multilingual learners that operates in tandem with the coteaching cycle (you may wish to retrace your steps in Chapter 2). Ultimately, we view collaborative instruction and assessment as vehicles to enable our students and us to travel down the roads to educational success together.

Collaborative assessment is not prescriptive in any way as it is compatible with a variety of curricular frameworks. In assessment FOR learning, there may be a schoolwide policy already in place for you to adhere to, such as backward design (Wiggins & McTighe, 2005, 2011). In backward design, assessment is front-loaded, so you and your students are aware of your destination at the onset of your travel.

In this three-stage curricular framework

- first, you name an outcome, the desired results at the close of a unit,
- then, you move to identify acceptable evidence through assessment, and
- finally, you design coordinated learning experiences for (or with) the students.

You may wish to pursue a more linguistically and culturally sustainable curriculum for your multilingual learners as in the EL ESPEJO framework, where components of lessons "mirror" those of a unit of learning. You should note how, in Figure 4.3, an abbreviated framework, these mirrored elements are unified through assessment AS, FOR, and OF learning (Hilliard & Gottlieb, 2021). You should also notice how unit- and lesson-level components are paired (i.e., 1a with 2a; 1b with 2b; 1c with 3c) to ensure consistent and aligned instruction and assessment. As in backward design, this framework has broad applicability across program models, curricula, instructional materials, and educational settings. However, the uniqueness of EL ESPEJO is its embedded linguistically and culturally sustainable practices for educators who work with multilingual learners.

Figure 4.3 EL ESPEJO Curriculum Framework: Abbreviated Version

1. Unit Planning Inclusive of Multiple Languages, Cultures, and Perspectives: Planning for Learning Around a Compelling Question, Theme, or Issue and Overall Purpose(s) for Assessment		
1a. Sociocultural Context: Community & Environmental Resources for Learning (Funds of Knowledge & Social Justice)	**1b. Language Focus on Genre** Based on Coordinated Content and Language Standards	**1c. Integrated Learning Goals** for Content and Language, including Translinguistic and Transcultural Considerations

(Continued)

(Continued)

Classroom Assessment AS, FOR, and OF Learning		
2a. Sociocultural Context: Student & Family Resources for Learning (Funds of Identity & Equity)	**2b. Language Focus on Related Sentences/ Phrases/ Words** Based on Coordinated Content and Language Standards	**2c. Integrated Learning Targets/ Objectives** for Content and Language, including Translinguistic/ Transcultural Considerations
2. Lesson Planning Inclusive of Multiple Languages, Cultures, and Perspectives: Moving Learning Forward Based on Feedback From Assessment		

Hilliard and Gottlieb (2023)

Briefly, in the EL ESPEJO framework, multilingual families' skills and expertise, in essence, their "funds of knowledge" (González et al., 2005), are brought into curricular themes and operationalized through students' "funds of identity" (Esteban-Guitart & Moll, 2014) at the lesson level. The genres or discourse that are embedded in academic content and language development standards for units are deconstructed into corresponding sentences, phrases, and words for individual lessons. Integrated learning goals reflecting multilingualism and multiculturalism of the students associated with units of learning match integrated learning targets for lessons. Assessment AS, FOR, and OF learning straddles units and lessons, serving as the overpass or crossing between curriculum and instruction.

Sociocultural learning theory . . . creates an imperative to deeply know each student—academically, emotionally, socially, and culturally—and to offer a supportive classroom environment where students feel safe to talk together about their thinking and reasoning.

—Lorrie A. Shepard (2021, para. 17)

Do you agree?

- Curriculum frameworks are most powerful when they are developed and enacted locally by teacher teams that are sensitive to the school's, district's, or community's multilingual learners and other marginalized student populations.
- Curriculum frameworks should not be rigid nor static; rather, they should be considered living documents that are systematically reviewed and revised based on student data, local policy, and best practice.
- Curricular frameworks, when informed by collaborative assessment FOR learning, involve input from you and your students.

We hope you said yes to each question! As we continue our journey, we offer you ever-stronger evidence for these claims.

Why Are Collaborative Assessment Practices FOR Learning Important in Our Journey?

They Unite You With Your Students!

Curriculum frameworks set the parameters for teaching and learning. Assessment FOR learning that is embedded in curriculum design helps develop positive relationships between students and teachers alike. Research on a whole school initiative on relationship building substantiates this point. Empirical evidence reveals that students who participated in this study tended to

- Enjoy school more
- Identify with and feel more included in their classroom
- Be less aggressive as perceived by their teachers
- Perform better academically than students in control classrooms (Miller et al., 2017)

In summary, purposely focusing on student–teacher relationships tends to improve the social and learning environment of classrooms.

A second concept that goes hand in hand with assessment FOR learning is that interaction between teachers and students serves as evidence for teaching and learning (Heritage, 2016). Finley (2014) describes efficient ways for teachers to use interactive checking or "dipsticks" . . . like "checking oil in your car" . . . with students. For example, students may take a minute to share with you something valuable that they learned or are wondering about, often using exit slips as a communicative tool.

Educator Promises for Assessment FOR Learning

Collaborative assessment FOR learning connects you and your students through a common understanding of learning expectations. The promises that you and your students make form a pact that is systematically implemented day in and day out. In making these promises, we ask that, as a teacher of multilingual learners, you do the following:

- You and your students focus on learning experiences rather than numerical outcomes.
- You and your students seamlessly incorporate assessment practices into classroom routines.
- You and your students exchange actionable feedback on instructional activities and tasks.
- You and your students' learning targets are matched to instructional strategies, activities, and agreed-upon criteria.
- You and your students engage in reflection, dialog, and decision-making.

- You and your students analyze and interpret evidence for learning according to the criteria you have set and then compare your findings.
- You and your students emphasize progress and growth rather than attempt to compensate for "gaps."
- You and your students plan next steps in teaching and learning.
- You and your students pinpoint strengths over weaknesses.
- You and your students become motivated to seek new knowledge, insights, and understandings.

How Should We Prepare for Assessment FOR Learning?

Through Collaborative Planning!

Instruction and classroom assessment are intertwined, so much so that at times they are indistinguishable from each other. That said, you have certain preparations for initiating assessment FOR learning. We offer you five suggestions, following your promises, as you move down that path:

1. Establish a safe and welcoming learning environment
2. Understand each student as an individual
3. Coconstruct integrated learning targets with your students
4. Match learning targets with student standards and criteria for success
5. Incorporate feedback into the assessment process

Establish a Safe and Welcoming Learning Environment

Before you can establish rapport with your students so together you can enter into assessment FOR learning, you must connect with each one on some level. As a teacher of multilingual learners, you may not be conversant in your students' languages nor have interacted in their cultures, but that doesn't preclude you from being kind, empathetic, and curious. It's human nature for students to react positively to nurturing caring individuals.

You should do your best to collect materials and resources in the students' languages along with their cultural artifacts so that they may feel welcomed at school and in your classroom. There is a growing library of bilingual books in many languages that are available through online resources. Colorín Colorado, a bilingual website, recommends booklists and videos for multilingual learners and their families (see https://www.colorincolorado.org/books-authors). Rotating displays of students' original work inside your classroom and in the hallways in one or more languages also sends a positive message, letting students see themselves.

Let's take a peek inside a classroom at the American International School of Budapest, where the goal is to create an affirming environment and to normalize multilingualism in the culture of the classroom and the school. Jane Russell Valezy and Lindsay Manzella invited all middle school students to contribute to a bulletin board in the lobby by creating multilingual welcome signs. During *Mother Language Week*, students were invited to share their favorite words in a language of their choice on this bulletin board (see Figure 4.4).

Figure 4.4 A Multilingual Bulletin Board Helping to Create a Welcoming and Affirming Space

Understand Your Students

While the classroom environment provides the context for learning in school, you cannot form a relationship with a student without having some understanding and compassion. Neither can you engage in assessment FOR learning without knowing your partners. Throughout the school year, you, your colleagues, and your students might agree on the parameters for discussion (as part of your language and assessment policy) so that your classes are comfortable sharing aspects of themselves and their lives.

There is a body of literature associated with the first of the six principles for exemplary teaching of multilingual learners of English, "Know your learners" (TESOL International Association, 2024). "Knowing" involves going beyond securing basic information, such as scores on initial screening measures or student demographics; it encompasses a multilingual learner's

- Lived experiences inside and out of the United States
- Social-emotional state (e.g., impact of trauma, mobility, stability)
- Gifts and talents
- Family composition and traditions
- Languages and cultures
- Continuity of education
- Interests and preferences
- Responsibilities outside of school (e.g., care giving, work)

This list is just the beginning. At the start of the school year, for example, students might create a personal collage or poster to adorn their classroom. They might choose to digitally record family members' histories and stories or keep interactive multimodal journals that are only shared with you.

There are several ways that you can collect information about your students to gain insight into their histories to help inform instruction and assessment FOR learning. You might wish to choose among the following:

- Invite students to produce autobiographies or family portraits
- Conduct a student survey in their preferred language(s)
- Make a home visit with another teacher or bilingual liaison
- Take a neighborhood walk with your class
- Take a virtual "tour" of the larger community with your students

The list can and should go on! Take a moment and pause to reflect on your most effective ways of getting to know your students and connecting with them.

When we visited Samantha Blanks-Gonzales and Ashley Rovner in their cotaught classroom in a suburban Chicago school district, something unexpected happened. Here is an excerpt from our field notes:

> *A student ambassador welcomed me to the class and explained to me what is happening! I loved it!! I have NEVER been greeted like that before. What a brilliant and thoughtful gesture, and from the students' perspective, it is an example of student leadership, agency, and an authentic opportunity to use academic discourse. (She politely introduced herself and ended by saying that I can approach her with any questions I have about the class!!)*

The rest of the class visit revealed that the lesson was filled with opportunities for the students to take charge of their own learning and for the teachers to connect with their students academically and social-emotionally. One powerful example is how Samantha and Ashley have a sign-up sheet posted on the bulletin board so students can invite their teachers to any sports, music, or other extracurricular events they choose. See Figure 4.5 as an example of what their sign-up sheet looks like.

Figure 4.5 Monthly Student Activity Sign-Up Sheet

DATE AND TIME	EXACT LOCATION	YOUR NAME AND ACTIVITY
9/14 5:30 p.m.	Middle school sports field	Carlos M.—baseball game
9/17 6 p.m.	Local YMCA	Annabel—gymnastics practice
9/24	City park by the school	Linda—celebrating my birthday with my family!

Building on students' strengths is at the heart of instruction and classroom assessment. Without having a positive relationship between students and teachers, the value of assessment FOR learning is greatly diminished. Classroom routines that depend on teacher–student interaction provide ongoing opportunities to strengthen relationships and form communities of learners.

Coconstruct Integrated Learning Targets

By now you must be curious about what we mean by integrated learning targets as the heart of instruction and classroom assessment for multilingual learners. In assessment FOR learning, you and your students codesign integrated learning targets for individual lessons while during assessment AS learning, students apply the targets in interactive ways to produce their evidence. You might wonder why we promote integrated learning targets over producing separate targets for content, language, and culture. Here is the rationale:

- It promotes mutual understanding and collaboration among content area teachers, language specialists, and students.
- It brings coherence to lessons by providing a unitary focus.
- It reflects theory and a body of literature (Mohan, 1986; Snow et al., 1989, as two ground-breaking publications).
- It is a Big Idea (content and language integration) in standards frameworks that overarches language development standards (WIDA, 2020, 2023).

As shown below in the shaded box, a formula might help you remember the features of an integrated learning target for multilingual learners. Hint: You do not have to replicate the order of the features.

An integrated learning target = content (concept or topic) + purpose for language (e.g., Key Language Use) + multimodalities + cultural referents

Now let's see what a sample integrated learning target looks like; here's an example for a fifth-grade classroom. It came from a negotiated discussion between students and their teacher that resulted in a week-long task (a series of connected lessons) within a unit of learning.

We will design healthy school menus with our favorite foods from different cultures shown on posters, in videos, photos, or illustrated text and petition (argue) for their adoption by the school using claims, reasons, and evidence.

Consider making some time to pair up with another teacher with whom you share multilingual learners to formulate integrated learning targets for a task that is based on an essential question or a theme of interest to your students. The target should reflect the language associated with a unit's content-based topic or theme derived from state academic content and language development standards. After you have collaborated with a colleague, bring your suggestions to your students to tweak or approve.

Our example of an integrated learning target for a task =

____

____

____

____

____

Match Integrated Learning Targets With Learning Standards and Criteria for Success

Learning expectations are generally grounded in standards that, in turn, are converted into integrated learning goals for units and targets for lessons. Applicable standards for multilingual learners include the following:

- Grade-level state academic content standards
- Grade-level/cluster language development standards in English (and Spanish)
- ISTE (technology) standards for students (and educators, education leaders, and coaches)

You may or may not be familiar with ISTE student standards that are "designed to empower student voice and ensure that learning is a student-driven process." In essence, these standards represent assessment AS learning that, when implemented with teacher guidance, introduce assessment FOR learning. In today's technology-driven world, ISTE standards are more important than ever, even if they just serve as a reference for your journey. You might check them out at https://iste.org/standards/students and consider them in your planning and assessment.

Once you and your students have set your expectations for a task or a project, you must think about the evidence or data associated with it. How do we (students, teachers and caregivers) know that the expectations have been met? In essence, this agreed-upon evidence can serve as the criteria for success. Figure 4.6 is an assessment FOR learning collaborative tool for the example integrated learning target. It is intended to be completed by a student and their teacher based on evidence identified in the task's criteria for success.

Figure 4.6 Assessment FOR Learning: Agreed-Upon Evidence by Students and Teachers for an Integrated Learning Target

The target for the learning task: "We will design healthy school menus with our favorite foods from different cultures (on posters, in videos, photos, or illustrated text). We will then ask our school to adopt the menus using claims, reasons, and evidence."

STUDENT EVIDENCE FOR MEETING THE TARGET	CRITERIA FOR SUCCESS FOR THE TASK	TEACHER FEEDBACK ON STUDENT EVIDENCE
	We created a healthy school menu (a product).	
	We included foods from our cultures (details).	

(Continued)

(Continued)

STUDENT EVIDENCE FOR MEETING THE TARGET	CRITERIA FOR SUCCESS FOR THE TASK	TEACHER FEEDBACK ON STUDENT EVIDENCE
	We presented our menus on a poster, a video, photos or drawings, and writing (multimodalities).	
	We stated a claim for changing the lunch menu (our argument).	
	We gave reasons *why* we need new menus (explanation of our claim).	
	We showed *how* we support our claim (explanation of evidence).	
	We summarized our argument.	

You may wish to take the integrated learning target that you have (co)crafted and deconstruct it with your students to produce evidence for learning, such as in Figure 4.6. You may also identify corresponding standards with your students and make them understandable through modeling. When assessment FOR learning is part of your classroom routine, students, with your assistance, can readily connect *what* to learn with *how* they learn.

Incorporate Feedback Into Collaborative Assessment Practices

We have research-informed evidence that "formative" assessment practices result in student learning gains; these practices include the following:

- Sharing expectations and associated criteria with learners
- Developing classroom talk and questioning
- Giving appropriate and timely feedback (Swaffield, 2011)

Furthermore, research tells us that feedback, not testing, is directly related to students' growth and learning (Arnolds, 2022; Black & Wiliam, 1998;

Hattie & Timperley, 2007; Schellekens et al., 2021). As part of the assessment cycle, feedback allows you to ascertain learners' progress toward their learning targets. In assessment FOR learning, teachers offer concrete constructive and timely feedback to students on their work. We can view and implement feedback from three perspectives:

- Student feedback
- Peer feedback
- Teacher–student feedback (O'Connell & Vandas, 2015)

When feedback is in the form of self-and peer assessment, we consider it assessment AS learning; when teachers are directly involved, it becomes assessment FOR learning. Features of effective feedback are presented in the following equation:

Feedback = praise + positive evidence + concrete suggestion(s) + specific action to improve teaching and learning

Let's unpack these four features as negotiated between you and a student:

1. First, establish a positive tone (orally or in writing), praising the student for what they have accomplished or attempted.
2. Then recognize what the student can do in relation to the learning target, giving some details related to the evidence.
3. Next, provide a piece of advice that is tailored to the student's strengths.
4. Finally, motivate the student to move their learning forward by offering a specific suggestion or two.

Here is an example of feedback from the teacher on a related activity. The integrated target reads, "We will use fractions to convert recipes to feed our whole class. We will convert measuring the ingredients from the metric system to the U.S. system and explain how we do it." During the activity, the teacher might say to a student, "I see that you followed Steps 1 and 2 of the recipe. In Step 3, look for language that *compares* the metric system to the U.S. system. What are some phrases you find? Use them in your explanation."

How might you break down the feedback in the example? Give feedback to your students using the suggested formula and guide them in how they might act on it. Then have your students practice giving oral and written feedback to their peers based on a familiar activity. Also, consider using technology to support feedback, such as having exchanges through discussion boards and offering comments on shared documents.

What Are Some Caveats/Challenges Along the Way?

Heed These Cautionary Steps!

The beauty of assessment FOR learning is that there are many possible interactions between students and educators, and each pair may choose a unique path to take. Classrooms may wish to take different stances that may or may not be fully in concert with school, district, or state policy. There are often two sides of assessment-related issues, so let's begin with those of interest and familiarity with your students (Gottlieb, 2022a).

Avoid a Strict Assessment and Language Policy

To escape the potholes in the road, we suggest that you be proactive with your students and colleagues to cocreate and share the dos and don'ts of a classroom or schoolwide language and assessment policy. First, let's start off with the dos:

You and your multilingual learners can coconstruct a language policy for your individual classrooms, although it would be more impactful if the entire grade-level or department team would agree on it. Whether you are bilingual not, you and your multilingual learners should decide the parameters of language use during instruction and assessment, such as in the following sample classroom language policy:

We are welcome to use all our languages when we:

- Think about what to do and how to do it
- Outline or draft what we plan to say or write
- Explore topics of interest
- Research to find out answers to questions or issues
- Talk with others with whom we share languages
- Collect and describe evidence for learning

You may wish to review what you might already have in place. Make sure that you avoid having a language and assessment policy that:

- You and your students don't whole-heartedly endorse
- Does not fully represent the variability of your students
- Cannot be adjusted to changing classroom circumstances
- Is not crystal clear in its implementation
- Has not been communicated to families in the language(s) that they understand
- Is monoglossic (accentuating English as the de facto language) when the student population is multilingual

A policy that you and your students codesign and adhere to can smooth out those bumpy patches. To formulate a mutually agreed-upon policy for both instruction and assessment, you and your students may wish to contemplate and respond to the following questions:

- When does the use of multiple languages enhance multilingual learners' access and opportunities to learn and show their learning?
- When is translation acceptable and when is it not advisable?
- How can students learn and show their learning through multiple modes of expressions?
- What role can or should technology play, such as generative artificial intelligence or other emerging resources?
- Does your language and assessment policy affect grading, and if so, how?

(Some of these questions need to be adjusted to the age and grade levels of your students so they can fully contribute to the discussions.) Upon reaching consensus, you and your students might then wish to post your policy in your room and share it with families.

The following chart shows one way to brainstorm the issues that might prompt discussion with your students and grade-level team, department, or professional learning community in cocreating a language and assessment policy. For each issue, you and your colleagues should generate a list of its positive and negative traits along with the potential impact of the policy before making a decision as to its adoption.

Devising a Language and Assessment Policy for Multilingual Learners

THE ISSUES OR TOPICS	ITS PROS	ITS CONS	OUR DECISION
Multiple languages			
Translation			
Multimodalities			
Technology			
Grading			

Consider Translanguaging As Part of Your Language and Assessment Policy

In collaborative assessment AS learning, we saw translanguaging as a classroom strategy between students. Here translanguaging assumes a policy-related role where students and teachers jointly pursue a mutually agreed-upon plan. In circles where there are multiple languages of instruction, both you and your students should also capture the metalinguistic nuances within and between languages.

Let's examine the practice of translanguaging, a natural dynamic phenomenon between students and between teachers and students who share a language. Its acceptance as an instructional resource, strategy, and policy should automatically transfer over to assessment. Figure 4.7 illustrates a range of possible classroom applications of translanguaging during assessment FOR learning.

Figure 4.7 The Role of Multiple Languages, Including Translanguaging, in Assessment FOR Learning

TEACHERS AND STUDENTS	MULTILINGUAL LEARNERS' OPPORTUNITIES TO TRANSLANGUAGE OR USE MULTIPLE LANGUAGES DURING ASSESSMENT
Craft integrated learning targets for lessons and evidence for learning that are attainable through multiple languages	Coplan with teachers ways to document evidence for learning in multiple languages (even if one or more of the teachers do not have full command of the students' primary language)
Have access to and explore online resources in multiple languages	Use multilingual web-based resources and research tools (e.g., bilingual books, websites, and podcasts) to explore content
Include linguistic multimodalities as a resource	Produce multimodal evidence, such as audio recordings, videos, illustrated digital storyboards, or labeled graphics inclusive of multiple languages
Interact in multiple languages during conversations and discussions	Offer feedback according to bilingual criteria for success
Use language(s) according to context, audience, and topic	Use languages of choice according to the situation

Adapted from Gottlieb (2023a)

What Do We Need to Pack?

Some Strategic Goodies!

As you and your students navigate the course, we are confident you have a sense of where you are going with assessment FOR learning. Several instructional assessment strategies are strong contenders to fulfill the promises for this stop in your journey. Let's begin with a sound universal strategy for all K–12 students.

Re-imagine Multimodalities for Scaffolding Learning

Multimodalities offer multilingual learners choices to pursue learning and ways for you to assist in scaffolding that learning by combining modes of communication, such as visual, speech, writing, gestures, and music, with text, which enables us and our students to interpret and represent meaning more fully. We believe that scaffolds should be viewed as building blocks that are integral to the learning process, not temporary structures nor add-on supports. Andrea Honigsfeld and Maria Dove (2022) describe nine dimensions of scaffolding based on seminal and emerging research and their field-based observations (See Figure 4.8).

Figure 4.8 Summary of Scaffolding Dimensions

SCAFFOLDING DIMENSIONS	BRIEF DESCRIPTION OF EACH DIMENSION
Instructional	Supporting multilingual learners through the entire learning experience by strategic lesson delivery
Linguistic	Supporting language and literacy development at the word, sentence, and discourse levels
Multimodal	Expressive (speaking, writing, visually representing) and interpretive modes of language (listening, reading, viewing)
Multisensory	Auditory, visual, tactile, and kinesthetic experiences
Graphic	Schematic or visual representations
Digital	Technology-based tools and techniques
Interactive/ Collaborative	Participatory supports to enable communication, role definition, and task completion
Social-emotional	Affective supports and relationship building
Environmental	Physical and virtual learning context

Used with permission, Honigsfeld and Dove (2022, p. 206)

Honigsfeld and Dove (2022) also suggest some key questions to answer when you and your collaborating teachers make a choice about scaffolding:

- What are the most urgent needs of our students?
- What is the purpose of each type of support and who will benefit most from each?
- What types of scaffolds do the upcoming unit or lesson require for equitable access to the core curriculum, language and literacy development, and assessment?
- What types of scaffolds do the upcoming unit or lesson require for meaningful student engagement in content attainment and academic language practice?

Scaffolding is integral to both instruction and assessment for multilingual learners so we incorporate them into integrated learning targets (see page 83). Let's take another quick visit to Johnson campus. The following mini vignette of a fifth-grade class with multilingual learners naturally interweaves multimodalities into their instructional and assessment routines.

Mr. Strom's fifth-grade class is tremendously heterogeneous, with students born and raised in the local community and refugees who have recently arrived under conditions of hardship. He realizes that the students, first and foremost, need to feel welcome and safe in his classroom and value each other's languages, cultures, and life circumstances. Therefore Mr. Strom strategically plans activities with his colleagues for students to interact and learn from each other using one or more shared languages. To enhance their understanding, language is always coupled with different modalities that the students prefer, including gestures, pictures, graphics, the internet, videos, and music coupled with text. The collaborating teachers also make sure that students can see themselves in the curriculum and their rich cultural heritages are represented in the resources used during instruction and assessment.

Multimodal learning can serve as effective scaffolding for empowering all multilingual learners (Listenwise, 2022). Figure 4.9 gives example activities associated with the interpretative and expressive modes of communication. The third column is intended for you to supply additional modes that are helpful to your students in gaining access to meaning during instruction and classroom assessment, such as in the example of different configurations of student interaction or the use of technology to support complex content.

Figure 4.9 From Mode of Communication to Multimodalities

MODE OF COMMUNICATION	EXAMPLES OF STUDENT ACTIVITIES NEGOTIATED BETWEEN TEACHERS AND STUDENTS	ADDITIONAL MODES TO SUPPORT LEARNING
Expressive (speaking, writing, representing)	• Describe and compare language-learning strategies • Present options for solving problems • Confirm steps in processes or procedures • Give personal opinions with reasons • Defend points of view • (Re)tell stories from experiences or text • Summarize conversations or discussions • Paraphrase multilingual multicultural texts	• During student–student interaction, e.g., in pairs, with partners, in small groups, or with peers, generating a graphic organizer

MODE OF COMMUNICATION	EXAMPLES OF STUDENT ACTIVITIES NEGOTIATED BETWEEN TEACHERS AND STUDENTS	ADDITIONAL MODES TO SUPPORT LEARNING
Interpretative (listening, reading, viewing)	• Act on feedback by teachers or peers to revise text • Classify/Categorize text by genre • Compare similarities and differences between shades of meaning • Show relationship between causes and effects in a series of events • Provide evidence from multiple sources to justify claims • Critique controversial issues	• Using technology-supported devices after watching a video

Adapted from Gottlieb and Ernst-Slavit (2019)

Next, we examine a strategy that has broad appeal and application but in this instance, applies to fifth-grade students, encouraging their deep thinking and discussion with Socratic-style seminars.

Socratic Seminars

Do you know that Socrates was an ancient Greek philosopher and teacher whose methodology has endured over 2000 years? Today, your multilingual learners and other students can continue this tradition. In fact, you might wish to regularly pack Socratic questions for your adventures as an assessment FOR learning strategy.

In Socratic seminars, initially you act as the discussion leader, asking open-ended questions, often based on an authentic text or digital recordings, to provoke student thinking. You should make sure that questions toward the beginning and end of the discussion connect to students' experiences to spark deep authentic conversations.

With you as the guide, multilingual learners might first be given the opportunity to huddle to generate questions in multiple languages. Then as a class, you can craft a composite list, such as the one in Figure 4.10. This joint construction of criteria for success can serve as the basis for assessment FOR learning. Students should then choose the questions they wish to pursue in the seminar and even practice them ahead of time.

Figure 4.10 Questions for Students That Typify Socratic Seminars

HOW WOULD I RESPOND?	POSSIBLE QUESTIONS TO PURSUE
	1. What do you know about this topic or issue?
	2. What is the background for this issue?
	3. How does this issue or topic personally affect you?
	4. How might you define what your idea means?
	5. What is a specific example of your idea?
	6. What evidence supports your idea?
	7. What might be a different perspective to take?
	8. How might someone with another language and culture view this issue?
	9. How would you respond if someone challenges your thinking?
	10. How would you feel if you do not agree with your peers and why?
	11. What steps might you take to resolve this issue?
	12. What conclusions or decisions do you reach?

Meanwhile, you might wish to convert the list of questions into a rating scale—for example, from a "thorough response = 4" to an "attempted response = 1" to evaluate individual students during the natural flow of the discussion. As students respond to the questions with each other, you might note their oral language, conceptual, and social-emotional learning. At the end of the seminar, students can self-assess and later use their analysis in a student-led conference, thus extending the seminar to include assessment AS learning.

Socratic seminars are a beneficial instructional and assessment strategy for all students. The questioning technique affords students opportunities to:

- Participate in positive learning experiences
- Actively listen for a specific purpose
- Stimulate critical thinking
- Gain self-confidence

- Pursue inquiry-based learning
- Develop metacognitive awareness

Let's take a side trip to Oregon, where Cindy McGean and Fara Musser Blaszak coplanned and cotaught for nine years in a third-grade classroom at Linwood Elementary on the edge of Portland. They frequently made Socratic seminars come to life in their cocreation of tools to assess student participation. As part of their Science/ELD lessons, students would record a focus question in their science notebooks. During the investigation, students collected data, drew and labeled diagrams of their observations, read related texts, discussed their findings with their groups, and answered their focus questions. They participated in Socratic seminars to discuss the answers they would write in response to the focus question and/or to discuss what they had written and added others' ideas to their answer. As students participated in the conversation and used pre-taught gestures to show their thinking, the coteachers recorded tallies and responses on the assessment sheet. The coteachers then reviewed the results during their coplanning meeting to help determine next steps. See Figure 4.11 for an example of their Socratic seminar student observation template.

Figure 4.11 Socratic Seminar Observations of Student Discourse

G = gesture. For gestures that fit in the stated columns, mark in column. Others, mark in notes. TP = teacher prompt

Group 1 TOPIC: Water on a Slope DATE:

NAME (NOTE 1 OR 2 TO SHOW WHEN STUDENT WAS INSIDE CIRCLE)	STATE CLAIM	GIVE REASONS / EVIDENCE	BUILD ON OTHERS' RESPONSES	ASK/ ANSWER QUESTIONS	NOTES
Sarita	1	1	1G	1	Needs small group practice
Matt				1	Prompt from another student
Lilly			1	1	Teacher gave prompt on a card

Which Pathways Should We Take?

There Are So Many Choices!

You should navigate collaborative assessment FOR learning with full support from school administration. That means time should be devoted on a regular basis, during grade-level team or department meetings, to allow for the natural flow of the instructional and assessment cycles. In addition, devoted time can be allocated for professional learning experiences and action research with a colleague for collaborative assessment FOR learning.

What Should We Do Before Leaving This Stop?

Reflect on Where We Have Been!

Guided by the collective voice of students and teachers, we have reached the summit of this trek. In enacting assessment FOR learning, we have:

- Determined and shared integrated learning targets with students
- Coconstructed criteria for success based on integrated learning targets
- Applied criteria to student performance
- Collected, interpreted, and reflected on evidence for learning
- Offered oral or written concrete descriptive feedback
- Made decisions based on evidence and feedback

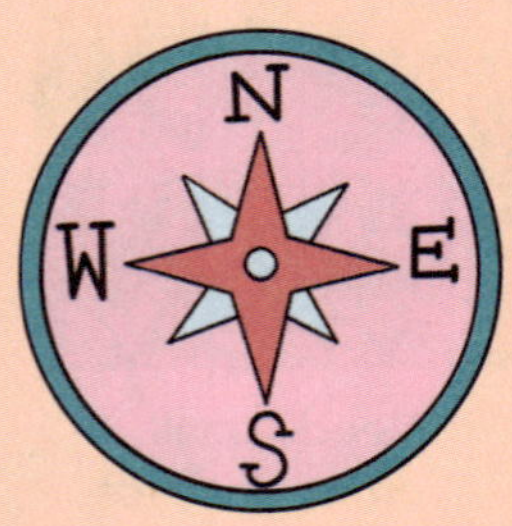

Effective learners will increasingly need to be autonomous and self-directed, flexible, collaborative, of open sensibility, broadly knowledgeable, and able to work productively with linguistic and cultural diversity. While still prevalent, it is held that standardised testing and a 'back to basics' approach to curriculum are unable to promote and measure effectively these skills and sensibilities. Instead, a broader and more creative approach to curriculum and assessment is recommended.

—Mary Kalantzis et al. (2003, p. 15)

During assessment FOR learning, you modify your instruction based on what students do while students adjust their ways of approaching learning based on your and other's feedback (Heritage, 2016, 2022; Popham, 2011, 2019; Wiliam, 2011). In this reciprocal process, you and your collaborative colleagues as well as you and your students respect each other and value each other's perspectives.

Where Do We Go Next?

Heading Toward Our Destination

In assessment FOR learning, we gather, analyze, interpret, and use data along with the learner to gain perspective, empathy, and understanding. In essence, this approach, along with assessment AS learning, humanizes the assessment experience through relationship building. In thinking of our collaboration between you and your students, we equate assessment as enduring learning.

"Rather than positioning students and teachers as objects whose value can be quantified, street data teach us to engage with people as subjects and agents in an ever-shifting landscape . . . it teaches us to be ethnographers rather than statisticians."

—Shane Safir and Jamila Dugan (2021, p. 67)

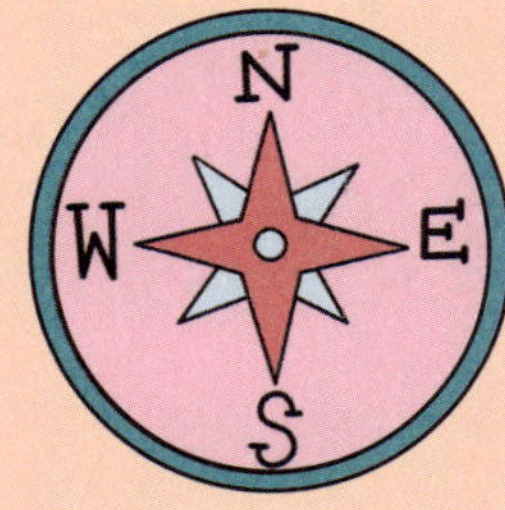

As you look back on collaborative assessment FOR learning, here are some questions to ponder or discuss with colleagues and students:

- How might you, your colleagues, and your students partner to form and sustain a community of learners?
- How might you make your feedback more concrete and actionable for your students, and how might your students provide concise feedback in a respectful way to their peers?
- How might a language and assessment policy solidify how you, your colleagues, and your students approach the multiple languages spoken by your multilingual learners?
- What can you do to ensure that collaborative assessment FOR learning goes beyond your classroom so that all teachers and students can embrace its promises?
- How might you share the formula for coconstructing integrated learning targets with colleagues and students?

Having traversed the highways and byways of assessment FOR learning, we have completed another segment of our journey. We have watched how students and teachers forge a bond through collaboration from a seventh-grade classroom preparing their portfolios for technology-informed feedback of other classes. Our journey continues as you team up with colleagues in cocreating challenging units of learning with embedded grade-level criteria for success for end products. So don't put away your bags quite yet. You need to get ready to discover how collaborative assessment OF learning complements the other two approaches to form a balanced assessment system.

Collaborative Assessment OF Learning

5

The journey of a thousand miles begins with one step.

—Lao Tzu, Chinese Philosopher

Where Are We Going?

We're Heading "Around the Bend"!

It's the end of the first semester at the Katherine Johnson campus, and we have reached a critical juncture in our journey. At this stop, teachers unveil a series of senior project choices for the high school students:

- A research-based capstone project
- A service learning project
- A career shadowing project
- An interdisciplinary innovation project

To offer guidance for their projects, teachers conference with each junior and senior to discuss their selection. Students prepare for this meeting by deliberating the pros and cons of each option, prioritizing their preferences, and forging their pathway to goal attainment.

Some students have interviewed Johnson graduates and summarized their findings as their basis for selection. Others have investigated the requirements of each choice on the campus website and evaluated the feasibility of each for themselves. Still another group has created a detailed graphic organizer to weigh the options and has kept a journal of their personal thoughts and feelings throughout the process.

At this meeting, teachers and students coconstruct a learning goal for graduation and review the criteria for success. In addition to their project choice, many juniors and seniors have selected to seek the Seal of Biliteracy as a statement of their accomplishments for having attained proficiency in two or more languages. This award is a source of great pride for many multilingual learners and their families in the community.

Finding Our Way

We might analyze this vignette as an exemplar of the three approaches of collaborative assessment. However, here we focus on collaborative assessment OF learning, as the high school teachers agree on four rigorous pathways for juniors and seniors to meet graduation requirements through a final project. However, in reaching their decision, students and teachers engage in collaborative assessment FOR learning to decide on each student's semester-specific goal for learning. Assessment AS learning is also visible as we observe students become introspective in contemplating their future, spending time to deliberate and scrutinize each possibility prior to deciding on their course of action.

In collaborative assessment OF learning, teachers form relationships with colleagues, school leaders, students, and even families to design assessment and deliberate data. The criteria for success associated with projects, products, or performances, whether presented in the form of a rubric, a set of descriptors, or a detailed project summary, are at the core of this assessment approach. Coconstructed by teachers or teachers in consult with students, the criteria for success serve as the template for interpreting original student work. Different forms of documentation (e.g., rubrics, descriptors, even test scores at times) are stepping stones for evaluating the data generated from the set of comprehensive tasks that comprise the final project.

Cocreating projects, products, and performances for assessment OF learning is quite a thoughtful undertaking. Following the sequence outlined in Figure 5.1, imagine how you might collaborate with your colleagues and map out what you might include for each step.

Figure 5.1 Classroom Assessment OF Learning: A Sequence of Action Steps

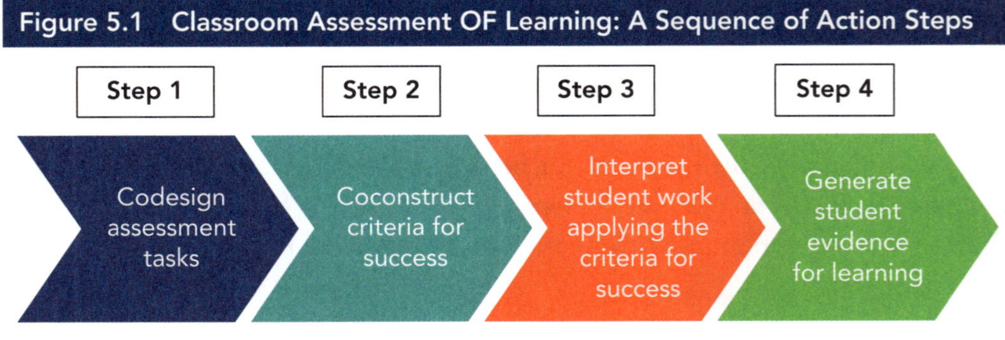

We invite you to pair up with a colleague or join your community of practice to discuss what is entailed in the sequence for codesigning collaborative assessment OF learning in your context at your grade level (as seen in Figure 5.1). What would be your choice for assessment OF learning—performance-based projects, traditional paper and pencil tests, or end-of-unit computerized assessments? In addition, what are the criteria for the Seal of Biliteracy in your state? What is the hallmark of your school's service-learning program, if any? Are there projects that are considered capstones of student achievement?

Once you have selected your format for assessment OF learning, you might cocreate a sequence of steps that makes sense for a culminating product, project, or performance. Finally, you and your colleagues might suggest how the process might be adopted/adapted by your grade level, department, or school.

We might travel a bit off road in our course of describing assessment OF learning as there is a wide range of ways to show evidence, sometimes as part of classroom instruction while at other times, quite divorced from it. Therefore, at this stop, we shall explore how data from classroom assessment can lead students to reach their goals while we also consider data from large-scale standardized measures mandated by districts or states. Analogous to Figure 3.1, Figure 5.2 presents assessment OF learning as a continuum, from measures that are within your locus of control to those that are imposed upon you from the district or state.

Figure 5.2 A Range of Assessment OF Learning

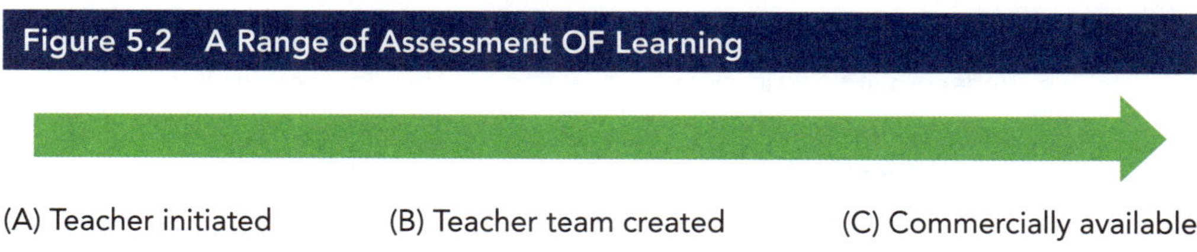

Assessment OF learning is challenging, with some demanding trails to navigate. Let's begin with how you—alone or with coteachers—might use a variety of measures to ascertain students' accumulation of learning, from projects to end-of-unit tests (that's A on the continuum). Ideally on this trail, you support your multilingual learners by integrating content and language in designing assessment, just as you have done during instruction.

The more robust measures, however, are those created from teacher collaboration teams, such as a school task force, professional learning community, or even grade-level colleagues, with input and support from school leaders. In this case, multiple relationships are formed during the assessment development phase through interaction with families, students, and the community (reaching the midway point, B, on the continuum).

As we move toward the end of the continuum (at C), assessment OF learning becomes confined to large-scale standardized measures that are locked into a school or districtwide plan. Figure 5.3 summarizes the types and features of assessment OF learning.

All data provide us with information for decision-making, and we have shown you viable pathways for making inroads to assessment AS and FOR learning. However, it might seem that data from assessment OF learning, from individual classrooms to the whole school or campus, are more heavily weighted as they

- Are perceived as "counting" more due to their ties to school, district, and state mandates and accountability
- Are more high stakes in nature with consequences (for you and your students) often attached to results

Figure 5.3 Types and Features of Measures Identified With Assessment OF Learning

	TEACHER INITIATED	TEACHER TEAM CREATED	COMMERCIALLY CREATED
Types of Measures	• Classroom-based assessment projects • Quizzes • Teacher-made tests	• Common assessment • Grade-level project-based assessment • Portfolio assessment	• Annual language proficiency testing • Annual achievement testing • Screeners • Interim testing
Features of Measures	• Mirrored in classroom practice • Embedded in the curriculum • Designed for educator professional accountability	• Associated with school policy & practice • Reflected in the curriculum • Designed for school/ district accountability	• Associated with state & district policy • Removed from local curriculum • Designed for district/state/ federal accountability

- Have extensive coverage (breadth) in topics or language domains
- Rely on a uniform set of criteria (or correct answers, as in the case of standardized tests) to determine evidence, across classrooms

To complement mandated standardized measures, we need data directly connected to the local curriculum where you and your colleagues have a voice.

Do you agree?

- The more classroom data we gather from linguistically and culturally relevant sources from varying persons and perspectives, the more comprehensive a map we will have of our multilingual learners.
- The more intentional we are about offering choices to our students, the more opportunities they might have to develop ownership of their learning.
- The more supportive learning environments we create, the less stress we place on students, especially on our multilingual learners.
- The more we can accentuate students' multiple languages and cultures, the more likely our multilingual learners will see themselves and become actively engaged.

What data from assessment OF learning are available to you, as a (co)teacher, a coach, or school leader? What decisions are made with those data, and who are involved? To what extent are you responsive to the linguistic and cultural strengths of your multilingual learners and multilingual learners with exceptionalities in planning collaborative assessment OF learning?

You might wish to add more specific information to the top row in Figure 5.3 to get a sense of the distribution of the different types of measures that constitute collaborative assessment OF learning in your setting. Then you might contemplate with colleagues which of the sources are most meaningful to you and your multilingual learners and why.

Have you ever found yourself a bit confused about assessment? Well, you are not alone, we have been there, too! Have you ever wondered where we are going with assessment OF learning as we are challenged by competing priorities and policies, forcing us to get off course? Let's just pause on our long journey for a moment and take a breath: We must remember the basics of assessment for multilingual learners and the promises we have made with our students in our pledge to assessment FOR learning. Always keeping in mind our students' individual portraits and leveraging our position of advocacy, we must ensure that our students are being assessed fairly and data-related decisions are equitable.

"In essence, we need to valorize learners' multilingual language resources and address the long-term possibility of developing language assessments through collaboration with teachers and learners in linguistically diverse communities."

—Jamie Schissel et al. (2018, p. 167)

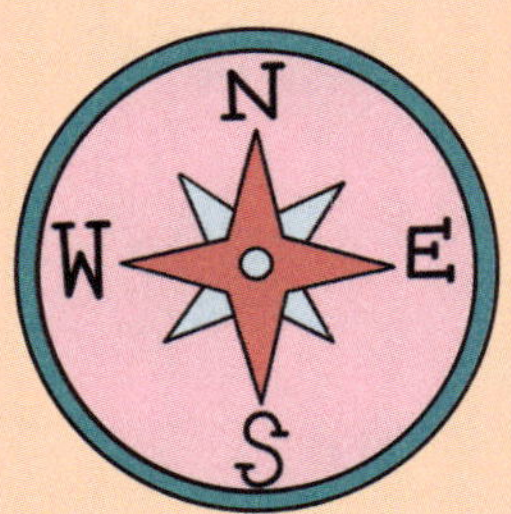

When we take out our pair of binoculars to better peruse the landscape before us, what we actually see in assessment OF learning is not a single approach but one that has been informed by both assessment AS and FOR learning. Figure 5.4 shows the interrelationships among the three assessment approaches, your and your students' roles, and the overall actions taken. You will be able to see the interweaving of the approaches up close with examples as we move throughout the chapter.

Shaping Local Accountability Through Collaborative Assessment

Do you realize that collectively you can make a positive difference in collaborative assessment OF learning by pooling your data and using a common set of descriptors

Figure 5.4 Spotting Assessment OF Learning From Afar With Views of Assessment FOR and OF Learning

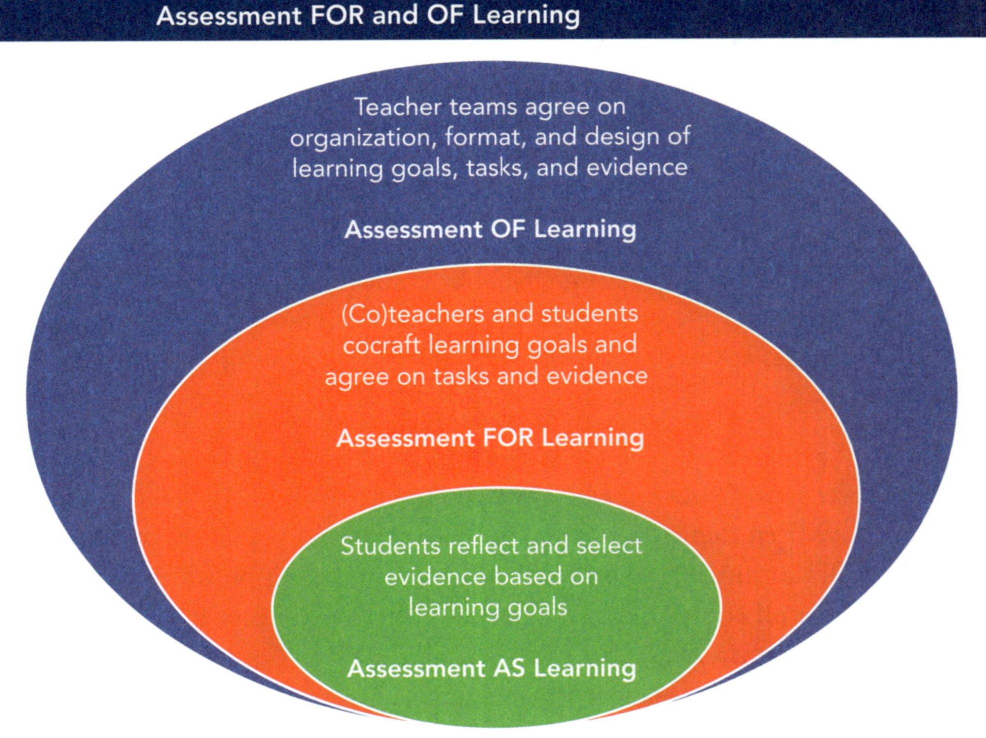

or rubric? As supporters of assets-based teaching, you are responsible for contributing to a robust dataset to define multilingual learners' learning. Therefore, you should have dedicated time as collaborative educators, coteachers, or a grade-level team to agree on how you interpret and archive student work.

Assessment OF learning is unique as the road splits in how data are viewed. At times, local classroom assessment OF learning is a stimulus for multilingual learner engagement, representing the interplay between content and language as a means of advancing student learning. At other times, data from standardized tools, another major type of assessment OF learning, tend to reinforce multilingual learners' academic deficits and "gaps," such as in the reporting of national assessment results (Gottlieb, 2022a).

Schoolwide agreement on the compendium of evidence to show student growth in linguistically and culturally responsive ways offers ammunition for multilingual learners and you to counter the ill effects of measures that are removed from your classroom values and promises. At this stop, we examine three student-centered sources of collaborative assessment OF learning; namely, student-led conferences, student portfolios, and common assessment, to bolster the robustness of classroom data.

Student-Led Conferences: Setting Individual Learning Goals

If not already in place in your grade level, department, or school, you should think about initiating student-led conferences. If you are already implementing this routine as part of assessment OF learning, compare our recommendations with your existing practices. These collaborative activities, generally occurring at the end of a quarter or semester, generally involve the classroom (co)teacher(s), students, and family members. There are several purposes for having such an event, the first and foremost to further relationship building with students and family members. Secondarily, as student and classroom data are shared to coconstruct learning goals, participants gain a sense of assessment literacy—a set of beliefs, knowledge, and practices about assessment. Thus, educators, students, and families can all use the same assessment information to improve teaching and learning at home and school.

Student-led conferences are an expression of assessment OF learning as they represent student work products accumulated over time. However, they may also be simultaneously seen as assessment FOR and AS learning; teachers generally facilitate these conferences with individual students (FOR learning), and students play a primary role (in AS learning). In this student-centered activity and empowerment tool

- Students provide evidence for learning and defend their stance
- Students are invited to self-assess based on their body of work
- Students show their linguistic prowess when interacting with teachers and family members

You might think to yourself that these student-led conferences seem a lot like a school's "open house," but it is more personalized and intentional, with students serving as the liaison between home and school. At student-led conferences, all persons engage in conversation (in one or multiple languages) to agree on student growth based on original work samples and collectively set goals for learning and plan next steps.

Let's visit Rebecca Gerding, English language specialist/instructor at Towles Intermediate School in Fort Wayne, Indiana, who prepares her students for showing their quarterly artifacts during conferencing with content area teachers. Spanning across four subject areas, students are expected to create an overall goal for the upcoming quarter using the protocol in Figure 5.5.

Figure 5.5 A Student's Guide for Conferencing

Language Arts/ Social Studies	Math
• Go over Quarter 2 grades in Schoology and discuss missing assignments • Show WPT Clash of Cultures essay • Show parents Data Binder in Google Drive • Talk with Mrs. Henry, Mrs. Kemme, and Mrs. Gerding • Show your artifact from Ancient American Idol in the display case!	• Go over Quarter 2 grades • Missing assignments: ____________ • Discussion points • Mastery checks for Unit 3 • Show your sticker chart • ALEKS pie chart • Conference with a facilitator

(Continued)

(Continued)

Science	Goal
• Go over Quarter 2 grades in Schoology and discuss missing assignments • Share your work • Monarch Butterfly Project and rubric (in Google Drive) • Conference with a facilitator	• Choose your goal for second semester: ____________________ ____________________ ____________________ ____________________ ____________________

Notes:

WPT = written performance task

ALEKS = Artificially Intelligent Learning & Assessment System from McGraw Hill (www.aleks.com)

Student-led conferences are not always a panacea, however; Kelly Cray, cultural and language support specialist from Burr and Burton Academy in Manchester, Vermont, shares her impression.

> *My non-ELLs rarely show up to conferences, so I have them create a presentation that is narrated about the work they are doing in the class and what they are proud of. I play that for the first few minutes of the conference as an introduction. My ELLs who have been here more than three months do the same video, which they narrate in two languages.*
>
> *In practice, fully student-centered (conferences) just haven't been feasible. It also isn't usually the experience my Hispanic parents want. They often will cut off their child because they want to hear from the teacher. So now I aim for a 50/50 split (student and teacher), which seems to make everyone happy. As much as I believe in students leading, I think the "business meeting approach" of the student being an equal and important stakeholder in a community discussion is also important and helps them learn to advocate for themselves.*

Although, perhaps, it may not an ideal experience in all settings, you should be aware of what constitutes effective student-led conferences with family members. Evidence points to the following features as yielding positive results:

- There are clear agendas and procedures in place.
- Students have multiple opportunities to reflect on, practice with others, and present their work to their teacher (and family members).
- Students rely on teacher guidance to prepare for the conference.
- School leaders support the event (Berger et al., 2014).

Interestingly, Lindsey Fairweather, a secondary EAL (English as an additional language) teacher at an international school in London, United Kingdom, asks her students to carefully reflect on their learning progress, the feedback from their teachers and peers, and goals they set for themselves (assessment AS learning). Although not formally considered a student-led conference that relies on oral exchange between a student and (co)teachers, Figure 5.6 shares the written interaction between a teacher and student at the close of a semester, illustrating both assessment FOR and OF learning.

Figure 5.6 A Student's (S) Written Reflection on Learning Based on a Teacher's (T) Questions

Term 1 Reflection

T: Which result are you most proud of? Why?

S: *I am proud of my Design work.*

T: Which piece would you have worked more on, if you could have?

S: *I would maybe like to have a bit more time on my science rapport* (report), *because I missed some parts out. . . .*

T: Read through your teachers' comments on each of your pieces of work: Can you see the same kind of comments repeated? How might you apply this to your work next term?

S: *I often get comments about (how) I need to be more concise or that I repeat some parts and write too much. I think this has to do a little bit with that I don't know the words to make my language shorter and more concise. Some words can, for example, summarise a whole sentence. To improve this, I will try to increase my vocabulary even more and continue asking my teachers for help.*

Overall Reflection

T: What are two challenges you're working through in English Plus?

S: *The past perfect; understanding the online comprehension program.*

T: Set two goals for next term in English Plus.

S: *Increasing my vocabulary using our online vocabulary program; try(ing) to make my language more concise and succinct.*

T: What activities have we done in class that have been most helpful to you? Explain. What would you like me to do more of /less of to help you?

S: *I like doing presentations and talking in class to [become] a* better English speaker.

Assessment Portfolios: Showcasing Evidence for Learning

Portfolios are a window into a student's growth and development over time. It is important to involve students in the curation process, allowing them to take ownership of their learning journey. By actively selecting and reflecting on their work, students develop metacognitive skills, become more self-aware, and develop a deeper understanding of their strengths and areas for improvement . . . portfolios can empower students, enhance their learning experience, and promote authentic assessment practices.

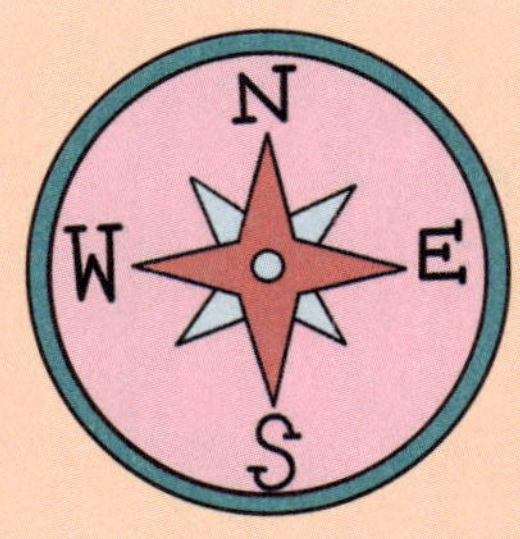

—Starr Sackstein (2024, para. 3)

Ideally, the data and artifacts that are shared during a student conference are a representative sample of evidence connected to the student's learning goals that are housed in their showcase portfolio. We do not have to blaze a new trail to explore student portfolios as they have been part of the educational landscape, even for multilingual learners, for decades (Gottlieb, 1995). While working student portfolios are useful for data collection, such as during a quarter, students should have opportunities to cull their entries at strategic points in the school year to highlight their accomplishments and convert their portfolios to an assessment tool.

Common Assessment: Highlighting School and District Strengths

Common assessment, using the identical means of collecting and analyzing data to ensure reliable interpretation across classrooms, is associated with a range of classroom activities, including multimedia prompts, end of unit products, or even teacher-developed tests. Common language assessment can be impactful, especially for multilingual learners as it should be the one place where you and your grade-level team can have agency in codesigning tasks and criteria for success (Gottlieb, 2012).

You can help elevate the status of local common assessment for your multilingual learners by being inclusive of their entire language resources (National Academies of Sciences, Engineering, and Medicine [NASEM], 2017), whether the students are receiving instruction in two languages or not. Students' independent use of their multiple languages and/or translanguaging practices are an empowering experience.

Let's take a side tour to Sioux Falls, South Dakota, where Sara Klaahsen, K–12 EL coordinator, shares how the middle schools have dedicated their efforts to crafting and implementing standards-based common assessment for multilingual learners.

> *Last year marked a significant milestone as common unit assessments were successfully implemented across all six middle schools in the core content areas. However, this achievement prompted inquiries about the applicability of these assessments to our multilingual learners.*
>
> *To address these concerns, the middle school curriculum coordinator and I collaborated to establish a committee tasked with formulating recommendations. Comprising of core content teachers, some of whom have experience with sheltered courses, as well as instructional coaches from each middle school, this committee brought diverse perspectives.*
>
> *Recognizing the varied experiences within our team, we first built background knowledge. We drew insights from the 2015 USDE Dear Colleague letter, the WIDA Can-Do Philosophy, and referenced Dr. Gottlieb's 2016 assessment book, using excerpts to enhance our understanding of assessment.*
>
> *Using a World Cafe model, groups of four engaged in reading excerpts of the book, posing questions, and participating in discussions. A rotating reporter system ensured participants had the opportunity to share ideas with the*

larger group. By the close of our time together, a consensus was reached on the standard administration of these assessments in all classrooms across the district. The agreed-upon strategies aimed to amplify the language in the assessments, ensuring that expectations for learning remained high for all students.

What are the sources of local data associated with assessment OF learning for your multilingual learners in your setting? Do data from student portfolios and/or common assessment help explain or complement results from standardized measures? Are your standardized assessment data in conflict with your local data, and if so, why? To what extent are the measures linguistically and culturally relevant?

How Will We Get There?

Carefully Following Our GPS!

Teacher, Student, and Leader Agency

What connects assessment AS, FOR, and OF learning is agency, as it holds the promise of empowerment for all who are motivated to effect change (Gottlieb, 2024). You and your colleagues can readily become change agents through your collaboration and interaction with others, making data visible and impactful. What is important is bringing multilingual learners into the fold, offering them opportunities to develop and access their full linguistic and cultural resources during instruction and classroom assessment.

"One of the primary ways students develop a sense of agency and independence is through language and talk. Talking helps us process our learning. Talking helps us connect with others."

—Zaretta Hammond (2015, p. 148)

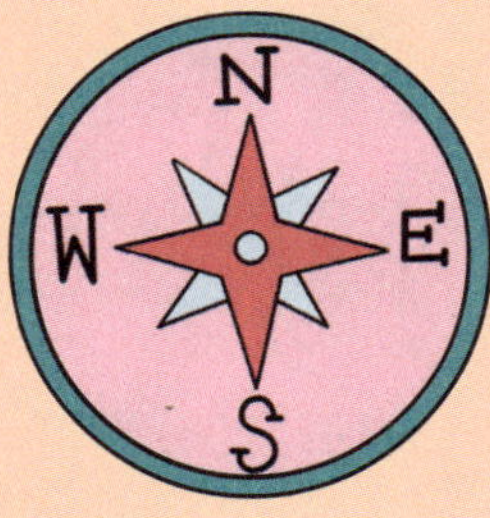

Assessment Literacy

What *is* assessment literacy you may ask? Who has it, or how does one develop it? Assessment literacy refers to your knowledge about the basic principles of assessment practices, consisting of the design and development of measures, the interpretation of results, and subsequent data-related decisions and actions. As an extension, language assessment literacy involves understanding multilingual learners' performance on language measures, including teachers' familiarity with theoretical and testing constructs, the application of this knowledge of language and culture to classroom practices, and paying specific attention to issues concerning multilingual learners (Malone, 2013).

Teachers, in particular coteachers, need to have a shared understanding of assessment (Dove & Honigsfeld, 2018). A whole school professional learning series geared to changing classroom assessment practices can build assessment literacy. Michigan has even crafted statewide assessment literacy standards and practices (Michigan Assessment Consortium, 2017).

If you think that assessment is complicated, so is assessment literacy! Simply said, assessment literacy involves a range of competences, including the following:

- Know-how of assessment concepts, purposes, and uses
- Application of appropriate tools for specific audiences
- Procedures for analyzing and interpreting data

What makes assessment literacy complex, especially for multilingual learners, is its unique features. For example, there are major differences in how we collect and use data from classroom observation, often in two languages, compared to that of state-mandated tests, generally only in English. Figure 5.7 is divided into two sets of questions to help you define effective assessment practices in your setting.

Figure 5.7 A Collaborative Assessment Literacy Tool for Teachers and School Leaders With Multilingual Learners

Questions regarding assessment literacy for **classroom tools**

- What evidence do you have that the assessment promotes learning?
- How does assessment accentuate the assets of multilingual learners?
- What makes assessment equitable for multilingual learners and multilingual learners with identified or suspected exceptionalities?
- To what extent does assessment evidence match the goals for student learning?
- How might multilingual learners' multilingualism be taken into account?
- How do you analyze and use data to improve your instructional and assessment practices?
- What is inter-rater agreement (or reliability) for common assessment, and why is it important?

Questions regarding assessment literacy for **standardized measures**

- What makes the test linguistically and culturally relevant?
- What roles do students play in the development process?
- In what ways are biases (linguistic, cultural, economic, gender) minimized in the test, or are they?
- Why should the norming sample for the test be representative of multilingual learner groups in your community?
- What are the differences between language proficiency tests and achievement tests?
- Which accommodations are acceptable for academic content assessments for multilingual learners?
- How do you use assessment data to make decisions about multilingual learners?
- What are the statistics (psychometric properties) of the test—its reliability (internal to the test or consistency in scoring) and validity (the match of the test's purpose with what it measures)?

The tensions of teachers dealing with assessment are palpable as they must be able to differentiate the different roles, purposes, and audiences of classroom assessment aimed at improving teaching and learning while simultaneously abiding by large-scale accountability requirements of their school, district, and state. The more that everyone is well-versed in fair and equitable assessment practices, where students and teachers are recognized partners, the greater the likelihood that assessment AS and FOR learning will take root as viable data sources alongside assessment OF learning to become a stronghold in the educational community.

Why Is Assessment OF Learning Important in Our Journey?

It's Based on a Long-Term Vision of Excellence!

Classroom assessment OF learning generally comes at the culmination of a unit of learning, where a final display of evidence is matched against the learning goal. In this assessment approach, educators often start with the end in mind. In identifying the end product, you and your team can then coplan, collect, analyze, interpret, and report information.

"Rather than view assessment of/for/as learning as hierarchical it may be more effective to view assessment of/for/as learning more holistically as more of an interplay of assessment within the learning environment."

—Dwayne Harapnuik (2020, para. 12)

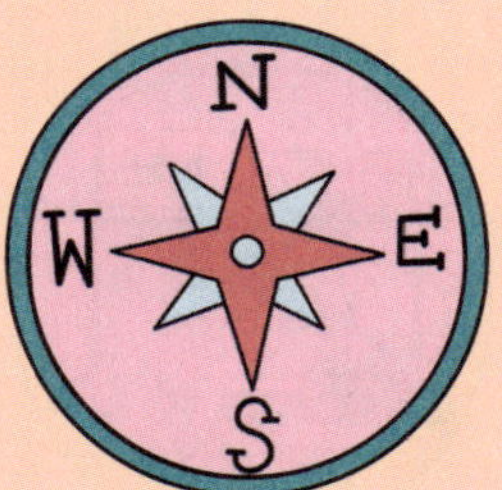

Although assessment OF learning is more directed to relationships among educators, we always take students along with us in our travels.

Educator Promises for Assessment OF Learning

In this assessment approach, you and your colleagues are the primary relationship builders and decision-makers, although multilingual learners are always on our mind. To establish and maintain a vision of excellence for multilingual learners for assessment OF learning, we suggest you do the following:

- You, along with colleagues and school leaders, have a shared vision of classroom and common assessment and a plan to enact it.
- You, along with colleagues and school leaders, support and advocate for multilingual learners and their families inside and out of school.
- You, along with colleagues and school leaders, strive for a culture of collaboration and shared accountability for student learning.
- You, along with colleagues and school leaders, collaborate in using student data in context as a cornerstone for evaluating school initiatives and generating reform.

- You, along with colleagues and school leaders, design and engage in high-quality sustained professional learning on relevant topics and issues (e.g., assessment literacy, common assessment, classroom assessment).
- You, along with colleagues and school leaders, have opportunities to coplan instruction and classroom assessment on a regular basis through pairings, professional learning communities, or communities of practice.
- You, along with colleagues and school leaders, are empowered through coassessment coupled with the sharing of and acting on assessment information.
- You, along with colleagues and school leaders, develop linguistically and culturally relevant assessment tools, along with your students, to pilot and use with units of learning.
- You, along with colleagues and school leaders, make decisions regarding the contribution of assessment OF learning to the campus's or school's overall assessment system.
- You, along with colleagues and school leaders, develop policies to ensure reliability and fairness of grading practices, in particular, for your multilingual learners,

How Should We Prepare for Assessment OF Learning?

By Responsibly Incorporating Technology!

Embrace Technology . . . It's Here to Stay!

Technology has become increasingly important to our professional and personal lives. Do you find yourself constantly being bombarded with new digital tools, apps, or novice ways to integrate technology into teaching, and are you faced with the challenge of creating new learning experiences for your students? As early as the late elementary grades or middle school, we know that social media becomes paramount for students, and no matter which pathway students decide to explore in assessment OF learning, the internet will always play a role. Most recently, generative artificial intelligence (AI) has taken hold in the educational community.

In assessment OF learning, AI should act as a multimodal assistant and a way for students to meet certain assessment requirements while fostering collaboration and creativity. As educators, we are becoming increasingly aware of the caveats that AI brings as well, especially in assessment, so you might want to turn to your district or state for guidance. North Carolina has taken the lead in releasing a guidebook and video on the use of AI in preK–12 public schools (see North Carolina Department of Public Instruction, 2024).

Students, teachers, and school leaders need some direction for how to navigate and use AI. We suggest that you begin with formulating an AI instruction and assessment policy with your older students for your classroom. You might wish to consider Figure 5.8, an example rating scale for AI guidance that sets broad parameters for use. Whatever is decided, it should be adopted by all students; in fact, as a class, you might even sign an agreement.

Figure 5.8 An Example AI Rating Scale for Instruction and Assessment

AI	DESCRIPTION OF STUDENT USE
1	You cannot use AI during instruction and assessment.
2	You may use AI during instruction and assessment for brainstorming ideas, giving feedback to peers, and producing final projects—if you state the AI-produced parts.
3	You may use AI for editing or refining your work to improve the final products, but you are not to add any new content to it.
4	You may use AI for certain parts of your tasks or projects and then discuss the AI-generated content with your classmates and teachers.
5	You may use AI throughout instruction and assessment as digital support for your work as long as you and your teachers have an agreement.

Adapted from Furze (2023)

Revisit Multiliteracies Through Technology-Driven Assessment

Let's admit it—our world is becoming more technologically complex. As The New London Group (1996) so eloquently articulated, multilingual learners are central to understanding multiliteracies as they are invaluable contributors to our growing diverse, multimodal world. Just as the Global Positioning System (GPS) has been a tremendous help in navigating us through our journey, other forms of technology have expanded our knowledge base and information stream. AI, for example, has been incorporated into assessment of multiliteracies and integrated into instruction for quite a while (Jacobs, 2013).

In assessment AS learning, we described multiliteracies as a personalized venture where multilingual learners couple their developing metacognitive, metalinguistic, and metacultural awareness through technological advances (for instance, students keeping a digital learning log, recording their own think-alouds, or reflecting on their learning using digital tools.). In assessment OF learning, we bring you, their teachers, into the conversation as you interact with different technologies.

Even before the COVID pandemic in 2020, technology was transforming teaching and learning. Today, technology is more influential than ever in that it empowers learning through assessment and shows the enormous capacity of multiliteracies.

Over the course of a semester, you and your students can engage in technology-supported assessment activities that lead to a final product, project, or performance, such as the following:

- Virtually observing student discussion groups
- Guiding virtual field trips (e.g., of places or museums around the world)
- Giving and receiving feedback on tasks (e.g., during posted "office" hours)
- Analyzing resources and e-materials for linguistic and cultural relevance

- Designing and contributing to classroom websites, blogs, or digital newsletters
- Using apps that stimulate student use of multimodalities (e.g., Prezi, Seesaw, Nearpod)

Collaboration among educators and between teachers and students around responsible technology integration is more important than ever. Figure 5.9 asks you some basic questions to answer with colleagues regarding the integration of technology into assessment OF learning; it also poses questions for your students.

Figure 5.9 Questions About Technology to Spark Discussion for Coplanning Assessment OF Learning

QUESTIONS FOR EDUCATORS	QUESTIONS FOR STUDENTS
1. What is the purpose for collaborative assessment OF learning, and how can it be equitably obtained through technology?	1. How do you work with your friends in coplanning your final projects? Do you all have the same tools and access to technology?
2. What linguistic and technological assets do multilingual learners bring to assessment OF learning?	2. What excites you about technology? When do you use it most at home and school?
3. What role does technology play in coplanning units of learning?	3. How do you use technology to explore topics with your classmates?
4. How is technology (e.g., the internet, apps, generative AI) incorporated into collaborative assessment, including the archival and retrieval of student information in multiple languages?	4. Which devices do you rely on? Which programs or apps do you use the most for your projects? In which languages do you look for information?
5. How does assessment mirror instruction during assessment OF learning?	5. How do you use your technology know-how to help design and create school projects?
6. How can multilingual learners' technological expertise contribute to assessment OF learning?	6. How do your projects show what you have learned through technology?

What Are Some Caveats/Challenges Along the Way?

Having Preconceived Ideas About Assessment!

Assessment OF learning often stirs up anxiety, in part, due to its tie to accountability. How can we diminish your concerns? We address six challenges in an attempt to soothe your angst and dispel any misconceptions you might have.

Mistaking Assessment as Testing!

Do you ever catch yourself using the word "assessment" when, in fact, you are referring to "testing"? If so, don't worry; somehow these terms often become entangled. Hopefully we can help you distinguish between them. As illustrated in Figure 5.2

(see page 99), assessment OF learning operates along a continuum, and toward the endpoint, assessment wanes and testing tends to dominate. To clarify the polarity within this approach to assessment, Figure 5.10 introduces a quadrant to differentiate the primary features of collaborative assessment OF learning from those that are more associated with testing.

Figure 5.10 A Frayer Model for Defining Collaborative Assessment OF Learning

What it is . . .	What it isn't . . .
• A shared vision of students' assets demonstrated with multiple types of evidence • Designing and enacting curriculum with end-products interpreted with uniform criteria for success	• Tests associated with district or state mandates • A single score for making high-stakes decisions • Grades for completing long-term assignments
Examples . . .	**Non-examples . . .**
• Products, performances, and projects at the completion of units • Rubrics or descriptors, applied uniformly to student work	• End-of-chapter exercises • Multiple choice or fill-in-the blank tests • Completion of sentence frames to form paragraphs

Privileging Standardized Testing Over Classroom Assessment

Let's face it, standardized testing is part of school life. With its deep roots in accountability tied to federal legislation, administrators tend to overemphasize the value of the results. Indeed, standardized tests offer a valuable data source about groups of students, generally on an annual basis, but to what extent do those groups represent those in your community and your local curriculum?

Ofelia Garcia and Jo Anne Kleifgen (2018) caution against teachers' and administrators' sole use of standardized measurement for decision-making, rather, "supplement it with their own close observations, performance assessments, and professional judgments. They should resist educational decisions made for emergent bilinguals that are based on one score on a standardized test" (p. 176).

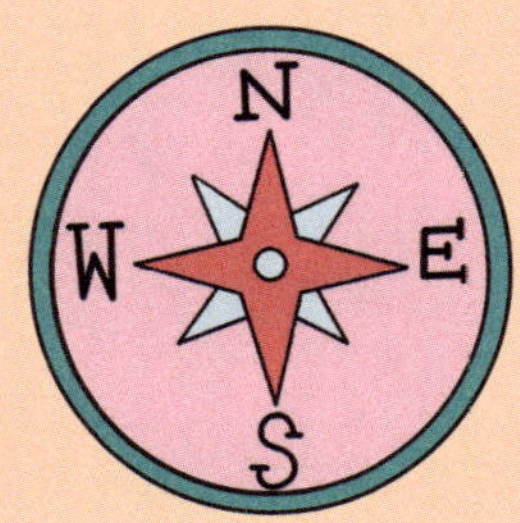

Multilingual learners, their teachers, and families should all become assessment literate to know what the numbers mean and contextualize the results. Here's how multilingual learners can be participants in assessment-related conversations about results from large-scale measures; simply look into how Holly Sawyer, an ESL teacher at Oscar Smith High School in Chesapeake, Virginia, has designed a conference sheet to discuss a student's annual growth on their state's English language proficiency test (see Figure 5.11). In sharing results, she encourages her multilingual learners to construct a subsequent goal for improvement alongside hers.

Figure 5.11

Name: ________________________

Date:_________________________

ACCESS Goals Conference! 2024

You've got this!

Proficiency Levels (1.0-6.0)

1	2	3	4 (4.5 Exit?)	5	6

Individual Yearly Overall Proficiency Levels

Year	2023	2022	2021
Overall			

Individual Student Report 2023

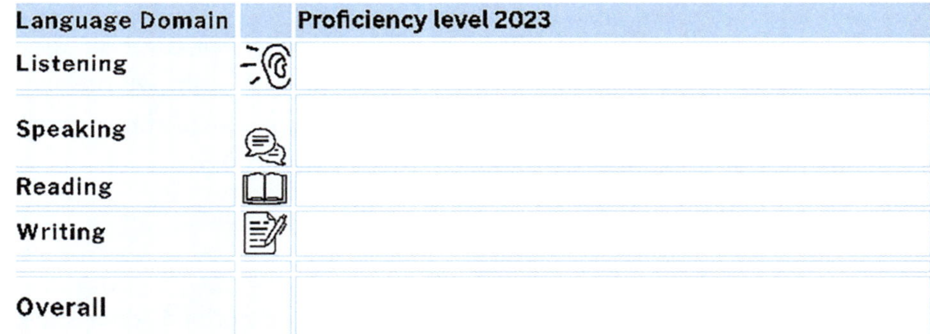

Language Domain		Proficiency level 2023
Listening		
Speaking		
Reading		
Writing		
Overall		

Conversation Points:

Let's set a goal for improvement! Which domain do you select as a goal? Why? How can you improve here? I also have a goal for you!

Your goal!

Your teacher's goal!

Engaging Newcomers in Grade-Level Collaborative Assessment

Newcomers may all be recent arrivals to the United States—however, they are as heterogeneous as the general multilingual student population with unique histories, languages, cultures, and schooling experiences. Understanding that trauma and other stressors associated with resettlement and acculturation may affect their learning more so than other groups of students, we must be vigilant and responsive to newcomers' social-emotional needs. In collaborative classrooms, social-emotional support can readily extend to student–student interaction and peer-led examples, facilitated by educators in multiple ways, such as the following:

- Establishing a dependable buddy system
- Utilizing flexible grouping configurations
- Encouraging and acting on peer feedback in one or more languages
- Creating a cross-age tutoring program
- Encouraging conversation between/among newcomers with a shared language and cultural background (U.S. Department of Education, OELA, 2023)

You can readily couple these ideas for social-emotional support with an assortment of multimodalities, maximizing newcomer accessibility to instruction and assessment while increasing their sense of belonging.

Assuming Scaffolding Is a Temporary Support for Multilingual Learners

For the most part, scaffolding for multilingual learners, originally theorized by Lev Vygotsky (1978), has been metaphorically described as a "temporary support" to be dismantled when student reliance on it is no longer necessary. The rationale behind "scaffolding" is sound—to maintain the rigor of the curriculum, insist on high expectations, and build student autonomy. Scaffolding is also considered a tool for equitable teaching (de Oliveira & Westerlund, 2022; Walqui & van Lier, 2010).

Given this premise, we take a unique stance. We say that most scaffolding, in particular, that which is multimodal in nature, is not temporary, especially for newcomers, but integral to and to be interwoven into instruction and assessment as part of the learning experience for all students. A prime example are efforts to convert STEM to STEAM. María Armstrong (2024) states, "We recognize and leverage students' artistic talents and interests in a way that can be used to help them connect to the world through math, science, and other subjects. It's about adults shifting their focus to teach STEAM through the lens of art" (p. 44). Art here is not seen as an adjunct or scaffold to facilitate learning; rather, it is a mode of communication that is embedded in and indistinguishable from the process itself.

Research shows activities using multimodal scaffolds (i.e., visual, sound, movement, text, and technology) facilitate multilingual learners' language development

(Choi & Yi, 2015). In fact, students' access to and use of their multiple languages is a multimodal resource! There is also evidence that written scaffolds specific to assessment tasks, such as rubrics and checklists, are effective in boosting upper elementary and secondary students' disciplinary proficiency as demonstrated in their scientific explanations (Kang et al., 2014).

Ignoring Reliability and Validity

If we wish to have defensible data for our multilingual learners, it must have two characteristics: (1) reliability or consistency in interpreting and reporting information and (2) validity in being able to draw sound inferences from the results. Consistency in interpreting and reporting student work can best be accomplished through collaborative assessment, where you and other educators agree on which criteria the student have met and which they haven't. Looking at validity, one aspect applies to minimizing linguistic, cultural, gender, racial, and economic bias in the product or project (or even test) under review. Another aspect of validity is determining whether the final product or project answers the essential question for the unit and is a bona fide linguistic and culturally responsive representation of the selected standards.

Confusing Assessment With Grading

Just like standardized testing, grading is a time-honored practice of schooling that is generally associated with assessment OF learning. Have you ever thought of the mental angst of students associated with both testing and grading? In addressing how to reduce student stress, Vatterott (2024) offers four shifts to collaborative assessment:

- From teacher-prescribed learning to student-designated learning (as in having student choice in assessment FOR learning)
- From traditional grading and assessment practices to student autonomy in grading and assessment (e.g., as in more feedback and negotiation in assessment FOR learning)
- From teacher-assigned homework to student-designed homework (as in practice for meeting expectations and goals, not grading)
- From lock-step schedules to the gift of time (definitely needed for coplanning and coassessment) (pp. 63–65) (parenthetical material added)

That said, grading and classroom assessment can move toward more common ground as, under ideal circumstances, both can be

- Negotiated by students and teachers
- Reflective of coconstructed student learning goals and targets
- Based on teacher and student feedback from shared learning experiences
- Markers of student growth
- Equitable for multilingual learners—sensitive to their identities, languages, cultures, and proficiencies

Which of the challenges we presented resonated with you the most and why? What additional pitfalls do you regularly encounter with assessment OF learning? How might you and your team resolve them?

What Do We Need to Pack?

A Couple of Bulky Items!

Data, Data, Data

Packing for this journey always begins with baseline data gathered at the beginning of a school year. Some information for multilingual learners is required under federal or state law, such as initial screeners in English. Concurrently, multilingual learners should complete an extended Language Use Survey that reveals the languages of student interaction with their families and peers in different contexts. It is also important to collect content-based language samples in all the students' languages to determine whether the multilingual learner is (bi)literate (knowing its advantages), whether the school offers bilingual/dual language education or not (Gottlieb, 2006).

We also need to take along with us student information that is being collected and archived throughout the semester and across the years, such as in student (e)portfolios. Additionally, there's all that data from collaborative assessment AS, FOR, and OF learning that reveal a student's learning journey. These considerations, along with individual student characteristics, need to be taken into account when codesigning goals for learning, assessment tasks and projects, and multimodal multilingual evidence to meet those goals.

Which Pathways Should We Take?

Ones With Student Input!

Assessment can get complicated! As we have seen, it is challenging when trying to figure out the meaning from all the information from assessment OF learning as it has broad coverage, from annual testing to teacher-created sources. Figure 5.12 is a flowchart of these sources of information that are broadly identified in Figure 5.2 (see page 99). In making instructional or student-level decisions, especially those that are high stakes in nature, you should always rely on multiple data sources.

Project-Based Learning

A classroom or grade-level choice that invites collaborative assessment is project-based learning, a series of coordinated student-centered activities around real-world questions or issues that fold into a culminating product or presentation. When working with multilingual learners, projects can extend into the home and community to welcome multiple perspectives and families' funds of knowledge (González et al., 2005). As a reminder, Figure 5.13 is a checklist of features of projects for classrooms with multilingual learners.

Figure 5.12 The Range of Sources of Data From Assessment OF Learning

Figure 5.13 A Checklist of Project Attributes for Classrooms With Multilingual Learners

The project is student-centered as it . . .

- Applies to and offers accessibility to the entire range of multilingual learners, including newcomers and those with identified or suspected learning difficulties
- Connects to multilingual learners' lived experiences, languages, and cultures
- Is of interest to or is generated by multilingual learners
- Builds on multilingual learners' strengths
- Ties to students' families and communities
- Operates in a context familiar to the students

The project reflects teaching and learning as it . . .

- Illustrates rich grade-level curriculum
- Echoes the theme and essential question or learning goal for a unit
- Represents an array of academic content and language development standards
- Can be accomplished a number of ways using multimodal evidence
- Lends itself to multiple languages, including the use of translanguaging, and varied cultural perspectives
- Can be readily deconstructed into a series of related lessons
- Is authentic with real-world application
- Has clearcut criteria for success

Let's go across the country to visit Hayley Naylor and Alexandra Anderson, coteachers in Meridian, Idaho, where their middle school students engage in project-based assessment. Figure 5.14 is a PowerPoint slide that outlines the criteria for success and describes a culminating project for a unit of learning. In this assessment OF learning example, groups of students collaborate to produce a multimodal comparative character analysis.

Figure 5.14 Directions and Criteria for Success for an Assessment Project

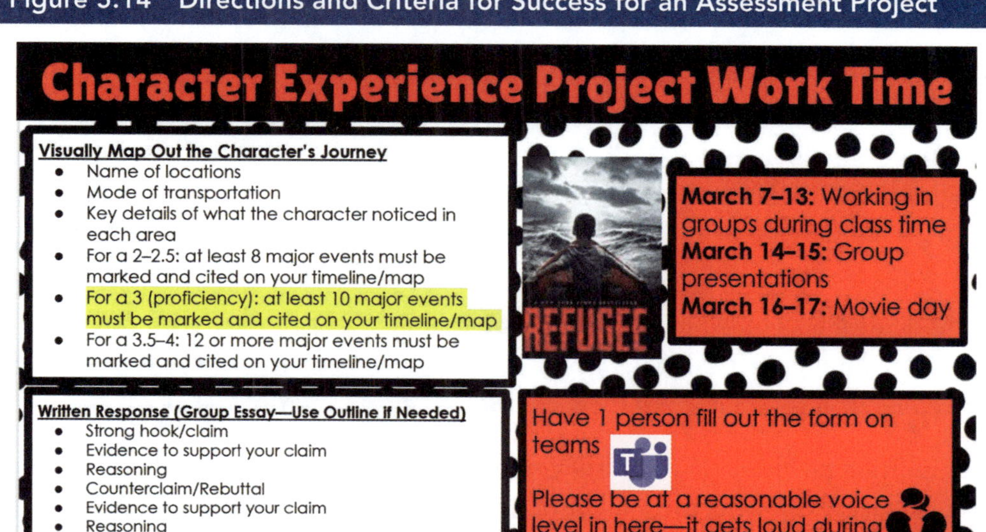

"The 'show me' approach to assessment includes (a) project assessment of in-depth learning tasks, (b) performance assessment of how students complete tasks, (c) quantification of collaborative skills, and (d) ongoing documentation through portfolios."

—Jon Callow (2008, p. 617)

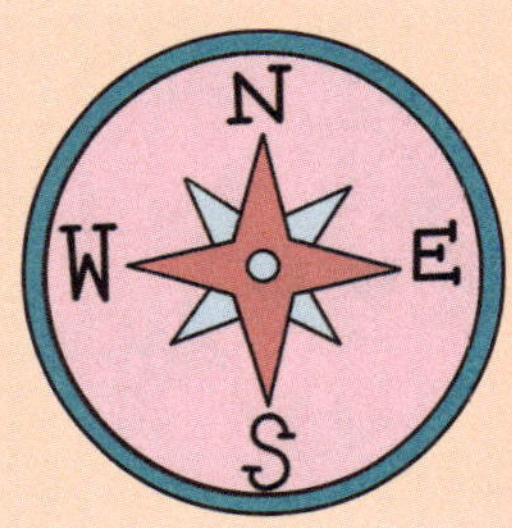

In our travels, we are going to take a bit of a detour to explore some offshoots of project-based learning. Here are three additional avenues to pursue in collaborative assessment: inquiry-based learning, place-based learning, and Makerspaces.

Inquiry-Based Learning

In inquiry-based learning, students follow methods and practices like those of practitioners, such as journalists, mathematicians, or geologists, to coconstruct a knowledge base, assuming the authentic role should trigger the students' curiosity and motivate them to engage in problem-solving using high-level questioning. For example, while science investigations spark student thinking, so do classroom debates where students have their choice of issues and positions to take.

What comes next in inquiry-based learning? The following four basic steps form a sketch for a unit of learning:

1. Students, in pairs or triads, develop open-ended questions, often around a topic for which they seek answers. They exchange their questions with classmates and obtain peer feedback. From there, they make revisions and identify a problem or an issue.
2. Students research their problem or issue while you provide digital and other resources in multiple languages and exemplars of possible routes to take. Acting as a guide in the process, it's your turn to give concrete actionable feedback to the students.
3. Students present what they've learned in multimodal ways and relate how their artifact or product meets the mutually agreed upon criteria for success. Students may even develop or add to a website using Weebly or perhaps a slideshow using Google Slides.
4. Students reflect on what worked and what didn't. Here is where you can work on developing their metacognitive awareness, asking them to focus on *how* they learned in addition to *what* they learned (Wolpert-Gawron, 2016).

Your multilingual learners may also wish to respond to how and why they interwove their languages (showing metalinguistic awareness) along with cross-cultural insights that influenced their thinking (metacultural awareness).

Which qualities of assessment AS, FOR, and OF learning do you see in these inquiry steps? How do incorporating all three approaches of assessment into instruction strengthen a product or project?

Place-Based Learning

Place-based education "immerses students in local heritage, cultures, landscapes, opportunities, and experiences as a foundation" for a multidisciplinary curriculum. Its goals speak to

- Student engagement
- Community social vitality
- Ecological integrity (Promise of Place, n.d.)

Like inquiry-based learning, place-based education revolves around interesting questions for teachers and students to explore, topics of importance to learners, and individual or group products. Place-based learning has great potential for multilingual learners as it

- Explores local ecosystem communities
- Acknowledges and utilizes the natural surroundings
- Invites students to learn about their home environments
- Accentuates the assets of multilingual learners
- Gives students opportunities to compare and contrast places of prior importance in their lives
- Captures indigenous or elder knowledge and cultural values (Gottlieb, 2024)

Makerspaces

You may not be aware of this type of project, but most likely, you are familiar with the concept. Makerspaces are a global phenomenon that has been emerging in schools, libraries, and museums all over the world (Hira & Hynes, 2018). In essence, students coconstruct and share their inventions or imaginative artifacts, and in doing so, learners become creative producers rather than consumers. You might say that Makerspaces are hands-on, often quite elaborate, student-centered projects in K–12 settings. Don't underestimate your multilingual learners; your students might surprise you with how sophisticated their products can be!

As Makerspaces are personally meaningful, they help support student agency, independence, ingenuity, resourcefulness, and confidence. Some examples of Makerspaces for younger students might be cocreating a community with blocks or a mural of natural materials, while those for older students might include designing and printing 3-D objects using computer-assisted tools or taking on robotics as an engineering project.

What Should We Do Before Leaving This Stop?

Make Sure We're on Our Way to Meeting Our Goals!

Folding assessment AS and FOR learning into assessment OF learning creates a dynamic and supportive learning environment for multilingual learners and their teachers. Understanding that data from standardized tests offer a narrow view of our students, we must redouble our efforts to be inclusive of other ways to generate linguistically and culturally relevant information that reflect our students and inform teaching and learning. So we purposely look at additional types of assessment OF learning, including projects, as contributors to the body of evidence.

Ultimately, we have strived to foster student self-awareness and empowerment, promoted their engagement, and built enduring relationships; all the while, we witness our students' grow in their language, literacy, conceptual, and social-emotional development. How do we accomplish such a feat, you may ask? We are always vigilant on how we might extend collaborative assessment to the entire educational community.

"Collaboration among coaches, content teachers, and language specialists forms a robust bond which strengthens the assessment expertise of all who are involved with educating multilingual learners."

—Margo Gottlieb and Margarita Calderón (2024, p. 53)

Where Do We Go Next?

Heading Toward Our Last Stop!

With agreed-upon goals for learning, we can forge clear and consistent road maps for educators, families, and students. When collaborative assessment practices for multilingual learners and their teachers revolve a common set of promises, we have definitive pathways for documenting content-driven language and language-driven content.

We have embarked on a journey to empower multilingual learners and their teachers with engaging practical resources. Beginning our travels with coplanning for both collaborative instruction and assessment, we soon realized that we also have unitary goals for both cycles. In the end, we reach the same destination, although the paths to reaching it are varied. In assessment OF learning, we survey how units of study along with their uniform criteria for success serve as viable data sources. With that in mind, let's reflect on how we, as collaborators and advocates for our multilingual learners, can elevate the status of classroom assessment OF learning:

- How do you envision collaborative assessment OF learning working together with assessment AS and FOR learning in a unit? When, where, how, and with whom do each occur? Is each approach linguistically and culturally relevant for your multilingual learners?
- How might you deconstruct the product or project at the close of a unit into varied multimodal options for your multilingual learners in a related set of lessons?
- Might you consider conducting an assessment audit with your school team or professional learning community to determine the extent to which the measures within assessment OF learning (from classroom products to campuswide standardized tests) are balanced?
- How might you set guard rails so that assessment OF learning, especially standardized testing, doesn't take precedent over assessment AS and FOR learning?

- What have you learned about collaborative assessment OF learning to better serve your multilingual learners?

Our travels have taken us to an array of exciting collaborative assessment places. We have journeyed across instructional and assessment cycles to optimize learning for our multilingual learners, providing you with strategies and tools essential for navigating the complexities of designing, implementing, and interpreting information from multilingual learners that offer sound evidence for student learning (Brookhart, 2023). As we have crisscrossed the country, we have become aware of shifting perceptions, as educators and students gradually take ownership of teaching and learning through collaborative assessment practices. Turning to the last chapter, we keep in mind how we might extend assessment AS, FOR, and OF learning beyond the confines of school.

Collaborative Assessment Beyond the Classroom 6

A driver is a force that attracts power and generates motion on a continuous basis.

—Michael Fullan

Where Are We Going?

We Are in the Home Stretch Now!

With the *Collaborative Instructional Assessment Initiative* well under way, everyone on the Katherine Johnson campus understands that collaborative practices, including collaborative assessment, cannot be implemented without a deep commitment and ongoing support from students, educators, families, and leadership team members. They also know that it takes time and perseverance to achieve sustained collaboration!

During a recent visit to the campus, Dr. Pérez-Jones, one of the regional superintendents, met with stakeholders at the monthly community meeting. She shared her perspective on the campus's progress on the initiative, listened attentively to concerns and requests from the school and larger community, and reiterated a shared belief:

It is evident that assessment has become systemic across the three schools on this campus—what an accomplishment! You no longer see assessment as an annual event, where you only look at numbers and make sweeping generalizations or tenuous decisions! Nor do you equate assessment with an isolated act, detached from day-to-day instruction or long-term curricular and instructional goals. There is a strong team approach in place here, and I want to recognize and celebrate your collaboration in envisioning assessment information as a pathway to teaching and learning. We are still a work in progress, but we have come a long way. Congratulations!

Dr. Pérez-Jones takes her visits to the various campuses across the large county school district seriously, and she sincerely enjoys her interactions with the families, students, educators, and community members. As a resident of the community and a former teacher and principal in a neighboring campus, she is deeply committed to remaining connected to local community organizations that support youth development as well as the teacher preparation program at the neighboring college. She does not claim she has all the answers, nor does she pretend to bring solutions to every problem. But she does listen. She is well-known for "speaking the language" of the families—and it's not just about her being bilingual; it is much more about her respect and connections with the larger community.

Some concerns and questions from parents and guardians Dr. Pérez-Jones and her site-based leadership team address on the spot. Others may require research and a longer process to reach consensus. Here are some assessment-related issues being raised:

- *Why do tests make my child feel anxious and what I can do about it? Am I the only one struggling with this? What can the teachers and the school do about it?*
- *During the state assessments last year, my child had several accommodations on the content tests but not on the English language proficiency assessment. I am really confused about the choices the school makes. Can someone explain this to me and my child?*
- *We are new here. I heard that the state tests are given in some of the languages spoken in the community, but why not in my home language? It is not fair to us.*
- *How can we parents help our children at home when we mainly speak languages other than English?*
- *Thank you for translating the report cards into Spanish, but I still need some more explanation. Please tell me what the report card means. How do I know my kid is doing OK?*

At the open forum, Dr. Pérez-Jones thoughtfully responded to the issues brought by families with tact and support from other educators, including the three building principals and the bilingual family liaisons. For those requests requiring a more systemic approach and revisiting of policy, she will work both at the district and campus levels with educators and families to collaboratively resolve them.

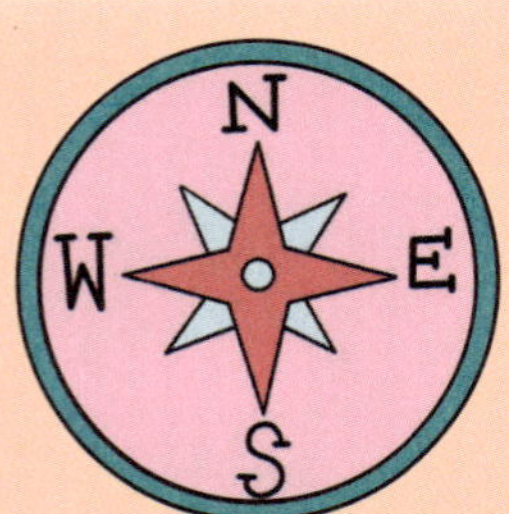

What Dr. Pérez-Jones believes and practices is often referred to as distributed leadership. It is powerfully captured as a dynamic, equity-oriented approach by Jeffrey Brooks et al. (2007) as follows:

> [Distributed leadership] is a fluid phenomenon that does not necessarily reside in superhero leaders who inspire those around them to rise up against inequity; rather, it may instead be something practiced between leaders and followers, mediated by the tools and routines that provide structure (and sometimes confusion) to these interactions and to the ways that leaders, followers, and situations evolve over time in a context. (p. 404)

Finding Our Way

After carefully looking into some rather complex dilemmas, Dr. Pérez-Jones gathered more data and feedback from the students and educators on campus. She formed a task force to investigate current, evidence-based best practices, and she reviewed federal and state policies and guidelines. In collaboration with her leadership team, she proposed some short-term and longer-term goals to enhance existing practices and continued working on a collaborative, fair, and meaningful assessment system inclusive of all stakeholders. Patricia Morita-Mullaney (2022) also emphasizes how this type of "collaborative construction among the ESL/Bilingual district leader, building principal, teacher leaders and families creates possibilities for *equitable educational conditions* for emergent bilingual students and families." We, too, encourage you to embrace equitable educational opportunities for your multilingual learners and families built on collaborative curricular, instructional, and assessment policies and practices.

The collaborative construction of educational conditions that forge equitable assessment practices, especially through family engagement, requires commitment and determination. Whether you are just looking ahead to this journey or already are traveling the path to collaborative assessment, take time to stop and reflect on where you have been and where you are heading next.

- Is your classroom, school, and campus (district) assessment system designed and aligned with your multilingual learners in mind?
- What are the signs that assessment is linguistically and culturally relevant?
- Do your multilingual learners have multimodal choices in selecting and showing evidence for learning?

Expanding Family Engagement

One way in which the Johnson campus has been strengthening family engagement is by expanding the roles and responsibilities of bilingual family liaisons. At first, the entire campus had one translator who worked only on essential written documents for the most commonly spoken language (Spanish). All schools have their own own bilingual family liaisons, who are so much more than translators and interpreters. They have become indispensable members of the school team with direct contact with families, acting as linguistic and cultural brokers, collaborating with families and teachers during school registration and intake assessments, making home visits, and building partnerships within the community.

Ann M. Ishimaru et al. (2016) examined how "individuals who serve as cultural brokers play critical, though complex, roles bridging between schools and families" (p. 1). They also noted that leadership "enabled more collective, relational, or reciprocal cultural brokering. These dynamics suggest potential steppingstones and organizational conditions for moving toward more equitable forms of family-school collaboration and systemic transformation" (p. 1).

Considering More Options

Collaborating around classroom assessment must be intentional and focused—not just when someone has free time and can fit in a quick chat about how the kids are doing, even though that is a start. You begin with one conversation, one collaborative commitment, one team, one school at a time. Just don't stop there! Once you are in motion, stay on track and keep moving ahead!

We developed an assessment road map with ten signs along the way (the Ten *I*s). We envision these signs being used in at least four possible ways:

1. As a guide to help you outline the direction of your collaborative work
2. As a self-assessment and reflection tool to initiate and expand an in-place collaborative assessment
3. As a stimulus to promote interaction and relationship building among educators
4. As a questionnaire to spark or revise schoolwide assessment policy for multilingual learners (see Figure 6.1)

Figure 6.1 An Assessment Road Map to Maximize Equity for Multilingual Learners: The Ten *I*s

For our travels, we need the following:

___ **Information:** Are all stakeholders informed about relevant policies and current best practices to assess multilingual learners?

How is information shared?

___ **Input:** Is every stakeholder group invited to offer input into what works with assessing multilingual learners and what can be done better?

How is input collected and reviewed?

___ **Inclusion:** Are historically marginalized voices and perspectives included in these initial conversations?

How do you make sure everyone has a seat at the table?

___ **Intention:** Are the goals jointly formulated and clearly stated?

How do multiple stakeholders inform the direction of the initiative?

___ **Initiation:** Are collaborative assessment practices for multilingual learners reviewed and piloted?

How are the initial steps implemented on a smaller scale?

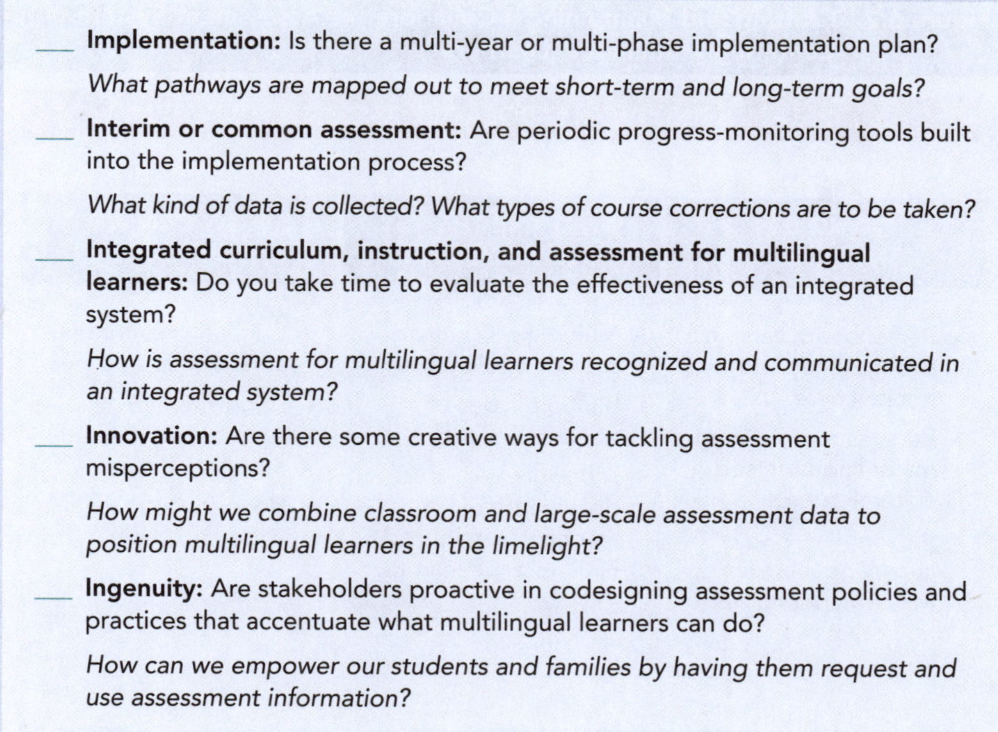

___ **Implementation:** Is there a multi-year or multi-phase implementation plan?

What pathways are mapped out to meet short-term and long-term goals?

___ **Interim or common assessment:** Are periodic progress-monitoring tools built into the implementation process?

What kind of data is collected? What types of course corrections are to be taken?

___ **Integrated curriculum, instruction, and assessment for multilingual learners:** Do you take time to evaluate the effectiveness of an integrated system?

How is assessment for multilingual learners recognized and communicated in an integrated system?

___ **Innovation:** Are there some creative ways for tackling assessment misperceptions?

How might we combine classroom and large-scale assessment data to position multilingual learners in the limelight?

___ **Ingenuity:** Are stakeholders proactive in codesigning assessment policies and practices that accentuate what multilingual learners can do?

How can we empower our students and families by having them request and use assessment information?

Here's a challenge! Take the Ten *I*s to devise and describe a collaborative assessment system for your multilingual learners. Share your conceptualization of such a system with colleagues. Perhaps you may wish to display your system with an illustration, diagram, or figure. How might you plan to implement it?

Shaping Cycles Into a System

A collaborative assessment system that serves multilingual learners equitably is built around the students' individual (yet another I) and collective portraits that are aligned to the three approaches to assessment—AS, FOR, and OF learning. It is characterized by multiple sources of evidence provided by multiple stakeholders or participants that contribute to an overall picture of what the students can do, no matter what their challenges, and what direction to take. The system underscores multilingual learners' right to culturally and linguistically responsive and sustainable learning experiences. With multilingual learners at the forefront, an assessment system must be stable, relying on the same data sources over time, yet nimble in being able to quickly adjust to changes in the student population, new mandates, or shifts in policy (see Figure 6.2).

Figure 6.2 Crafting and Maintaining a Collaborative Assessment System Centering Multilingual Learners

ESTABLISHING A COLLABORATIVE ASSESSMENT SYSTEM

WHO IS INVOLVED?	WHAT ARE THE KEY COMPONENTS?	HOW CAN WE ENSURE EQUITY?
• Persons with varying backgrounds and perspectives • Persons representing major linguistic and cultural groups • Persons knowledgeable in assessment policies and practices	• Multiple qualitative sources of evidence • Multiple types of quantitative data • A balance of documentation among assessment AS, FOR, and OF learning	• Culturally responsive assessment practices • Linguistically sustainable assessment tools • Honoring student voice and choice

ANCHORED IN MULTILINGUAL STUDENTS' ASSETS

Linda Darling-Hammond et al. (2020) remind us to consider all aspects of the educational environment and all dimensions of students' developmental experiences in designing a sound and functional system:

> This calls for a deeply integrated approach to practice that supports the whole child in schools and classrooms that function coherently and consistently to build strong relationships and learning communities; support social, emotional, and cognitive development; and provide a system of supports as needed for healthy development, productive relationships, and academic progress. This holistic approach must necessarily connect with family and community contexts: developing strong, respectful partnerships to understand and build on children's experiences and, as needed, to strengthen any aspects of the developmental system where there are challenges to children's health and well-being. (pp. 98–99)

How Will We Get There?

Multilingual Students, Families, and Educators Map Out the Final Leg of the Journey Together!

At this final stop in our journey, we invite you to go beyond the day-to-day in-class practices of assessment AS, FOR, and OF learning and consider forging partnerships with a range of educators and services providers, coaches, leaders, and families.

We continue to urge every member of your school community to take a multilingual turn (May, 2014) and adhere to multiliteracies as a principled pathway to student success in today's technologically dependent world. We illustrate how our collaborative assessment model and cycle are anchored in multilingual learners' and their families' linguistic and cultural assets to be adopted by schools—and districtwide. We also advocate for a systemic approach to collaboration, with emphasis on coassessment. As we come to the end the book, we hope to send you off on your own journey to advance collaborative assessment centered on multilingual learners in classroom and school settings with strong family engagement and joint professional learning.

Family Engagement

An important relationship to be nurtured throughout school and extended to home and the community is that with families. Maintaining open, two-way communication recognizes families as active partners in their children's learning and welcomes family expertise. Ultimately, strong home–school connections relate to positive learning experiences for multilingual learners (Jeynes, 2012).

Let's agree that forming connections between families and teachers and between teachers and students, starting in the students' early years, are foundational for promoting (and documenting) their academic, language, and social-emotional development (CCNetwork, 2023). In school and home environments, we encourage collaborative practices to be enacted on multiple levels for multiple purposes:

- Families and teachers collaborate—to build rapport, offer mutual support, and share resources
- Families, teachers, and family liaisons collaborate—to ensure productive two-way communication
- Students within a classroom community of learners collaborate—to foster respect, create comradery, and promote positive linguistic and cultural exchanges among classmates
- Students collaborate with teachers—to give and use assets-based feedback in productive ways within a trusting, caring environment
- Teachers collaborate with other teachers—to agree upon and implement sound assessment practices
- Teachers collaborate with coaches—to stimulate communities of practice around assessment issues, analyze and use common assessment data, and attend to multilingual learners
- Teachers collaborate with school administrators—to inform and contribute to decision-making and schoolwide policies.

It has been widely recognized that family engagement is an essential component of our students' education. But have you thought of how to define "family" in the context of multilingual learners? The nuclear family of parents and children might be rather limiting. We need to include extended family members, grandparents, uncles and aunts, guardians, siblings, or step siblings. In many situations, family friends and close neighbors may also play an important role in your students' lives. What do you know about your students' families? What would you like to know to connect with them better? How can you truly engage them in instructional and assessment decisions in school as well as in practices that reach beyond school?

Joint Professional Learning

To initiate and sustain professional learning that supports collaborative assessment practices, you need to establish a core structure for participation. As members of the school community, you may form or join smaller or larger groups to participate in a range of professional learning activities. It is essential that your district, campus, or school not only cocreates professional learning opportunities about collaborative assessment but also supports educator agency and teacher leadership. Figure 6.3 identifies possible organizational designs for professional learning practices around assessment. As you review this summary chart, consider additional possibilities for collaborative professional learning and add your ideas to the final column.

Figure 6.3 Organizational Options for Collaborative Models of Professional Learning

WHO PARTICIPATES?	WHAT IS THE OVERARCHING PROFESSIONAL PRACTICE?	HOW ARE EDUCATORS ENGAGED IN COLLABORATIVE ASSESSMENT?	WHAT ARE SOME ADDITIONAL POSSIBILITIES IN YOUR SETTING?
District or campus-wide participation	Equity audit	All district members participate in a self-study of assessment practices to identify areas of strengths and needs	
Whole school participation	Research and development; assessment literacy	All school members delve into the professional literature about specific areas of assessment	
School-based small-group participation	Collaborative inquiry (or variations, such as independent study groups, collegial circles, lesson study groups)	Individual groups set procedures typically consisting of • Identifying a challenging, pertinent issue • Reviewing the literature • Examining the data • Determining and implementing a course of action	
Two- or three-member partnerships	Peer observations, collaborative coaching, and mentoring	Each partnership team independently determines the focus of their own professional learning about assessment	

Let's return to the international school in Vietnam, where Ceci Gómez-Galvez and her colleagues engage in on-going professional learning connected to collaborative assessment. See Figure 6.4 for a typical schedule of their half-day professional learning session that focuses on (a) building a shared understanding of students' language proficiency levels and assessment of expressive language, (b) determining language proficiencies for speaking and writing, and (c) gathering and reviewing data for helping the team transition students to the next grade level and more successfully plan.

Figure 6.4 Coassessment Outline for a Professional Learning Session

TIME	AGENDA	NOTES
12:30 p.m.	Connections/Centering	
12:45 p.m.	Go over Agenda, Objectives & Norms of Collaboration	
12:50 p.m.	Co-presented by EAL Team • Building a shared understanding • How to use the rubrics	Reviewing Toolkit • WIDA rubrics • Sample writing
1:15 p.m.	Break	
1:30 p.m.	Writing Coassessment	With a partner/triad, coassess your students' writing samples.
2:15 p.m.	Break	
2:30 p.m.	Speaking Coassessment	With a partner/triad, coassess your students' speaking samples.
3:15 p.m.	Teachers co-reflect on the following questions: • **Connect:** How are the ideas, concepts, strategies, and so forth, that you learned today connected to what you already knew or believed? • **Extend:** What new ideas, concepts, and strategies have pushed or extended your thinking? • **Challenge:** What is now challenging your thinking? What questions or puzzles do you now have?	

Why Is Expanding Collaborative Assessment Beyond the Classroom Important in Our Journey?

It's All Hands on Deck!

Long gone are the days when assessment was confined to weekly quizzes and grade books. The dynamic collaborative approach to assessment we have been advocating for is intertwined with planning and instruction while it intentionally centers multilingual students' complex identities, rich cultural heritages, unique gifts and talents, and in and out-of-school experiences. The comprehensive nature of assessment requires information that extends beyond the walls of the classroom and the boundaries of the campus.

Educator Promises for Expanding Collaborative Assessment Beyond the Classroom

To fully understand our students and to best prepare them for their futures, collaborative assessment should capture data outside the confines of schooling. As you continue on your journey with us, we invite you as an educator of multilingual learners, to do the following:

- You along with your students' families partner to make assessment a shared endeavor. Together, consider
  - Setting shared goals for learning
  - Regularly reviewing each child's academic and social-emotional progress
  - Seeing language and literacy development through the lens of the student's cultural and linguistic heritage
  - Ensuring students and families have ownership of the assessment system
- You along with your instructional coaches look at evidence for student learning, set clear learning expectations and success criteria, and establish continuous improvement goals both for student and teacher learning.
- You along with your grade-level team leaders or department chairs examine the impact of common assessment across classrooms.
- You along with fellow teacher leaders codevelop assessment measures and tools and establish clear criteria for success to facilitate "I can" statements with all your students.
- You along with your building administrators determine professional learning needs around collaborative instructional and assessment practices that emphasize using data that are meaningful for students, teachers, and families.
- You along with your campus or district administrators work toward advocacy for fair and equitable assessment practices.
- You along with members of the immediate school community and larger neighborhood community create meaningful opportunities for students to share their learning in authentic ways and make a difference in the community.
- You along with local college and university faculty create pathways for preservice and inservice teachers to jointly learn about collaborative assessment practices in classes and field work.

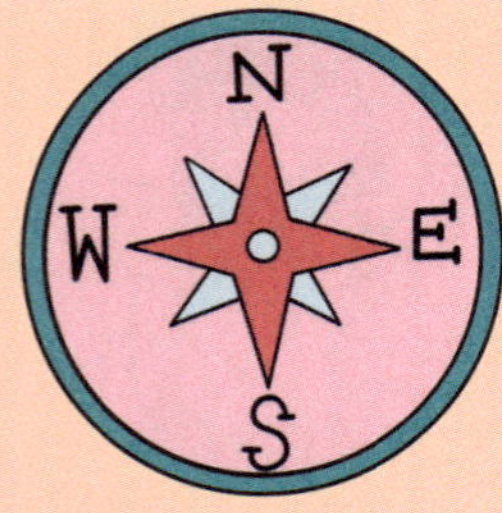

When using student and/or family voice strategies, it is important for teachers to foster a safe, open environment where all students and families can:

- Understand the purpose of sharing their voice
- Authentically share their voice
- Feel that their voice is being heard and will lead to action
- Have multiple and different opportunities to share their voice

(IES REL Pacific, 2024, p. 1)

Let's visit with Alexis Kiana Ortega, who is the managing director of the English Learner Department at Acero Schools of Chicago:

> *I have the privilege of developing opportunities for stakeholder collaboration in assessment creation for multilingual learners. Acero Schools of Chicago has partnered with Paridad Education Consulting to integrate the EL ESPEJO curricular framework within our planning template because it consolidates our must-have planning components while factoring in school-based curricula and supplemental resources. Within the Acero Schools planning template, there are color-coded features for sheltered English instruction, English as a second language instruction, and native language instruction that allow for collaboration between all teachers, regardless of endorsement, to focus on the features that they are certified to teach. Having a shared network planning template ensures joint responsibility as it pertains to assessments because it allows educators to frame students' learning experiences to point toward wanted outcomes while incorporating their sociocultural context. It is essential to embed appropriate, reliable, and valid expectations for what students will process and produce for assessment purposes as it relates to their language abilities. Assessments OF learning utilize language as the driving force toward mirroring AS and FOR learning assessments. Dedicating network professional development sessions to building teacher-led co-curated biliteracy units of study allows assessment criteria for success to be used as a lever and an integral part of backward designing plans to develop language and content simultaneously. Through collaborative work, teachers maximize their strengths and build a sense of ownership of our network's overarching goal of holistic instruction and assessment implementation.*

How Should We Prepare for Collaborative Assessment That Goes Beyond the Classroom?

Having Students, Educators, and Families Use the Right Drivers

As we demonstrated in the first five chapters, planning and implementing the collaborative assessment cycle within the classroom are powerful practices. Taking collaborative assessment beyond the classroom can be truly transformational . . . but easier said than done! Have you thought about what drives educational change? What leads to a lasting impact on student learning?

Inspired by Michael Fullan and Joanne Quinn's (2024) vision of transforming learning, we have identified four drivers—powerful sets of actions that move together to propel us forward. When these four drivers work in sync with each other, we begin to shift our thinking. See if you agree with us!

Driver 1: Encouraging life-long, active learning through collaborative practices among stakeholders—students, educators, and families

Why is this a key driver for collaborative assessment?

One of the most dangerous things to say is, "We have always done it this way!" With our local and global realities constantly changing, learning can never stop. If you truly seek agency for you and your students, your voices and opinions must be respected and considered viable options. Collaborative assessment requires all participants to contribute to and be vested in the process.

How can we activate this driver?

- Conduct needs assessments
- Form professional learning communities
- Stay informed and engaged
- Share what you know and find out what others have to offer
- Ask questions and seek various possible answers
- Explore multiple pathways
- Consider multiple options and take risks
- Advocate for what is fair and equitable
- Listen to students and families, then act on their recommendations
- Involve multilingual learners and families in decision-making

Driver 2: Harnessing the collective intelligence (CQ) that potentially exists in every school and community through the gifts, talents, and assets of students, educators, and families

Why is this a key driver for collaborative assessment?

Have you ever walked into a room and simply felt the place pulsating with energy? In every school, there is a tremendous amount of knowledge, skills, and experience that have accumulated over the course of the years or—at times—generations. The challenge and opportunity are to create cohesion and unity within the system by establishing shared goals, agreeing on values and beliefs, and collectively deciding on necessary adjustments to make.

How can we activate this driver?

- Discover and utilize the unique talents and skills of members of the school and community

- Recognize, value, and consistently build on the cultural, linguistic, and academic strengths of students, their families, and your faculty
- Attend to multilingual learners' social and emotional learning along with their literacy and language development to maximize their motivation and engagement
- Offer multilingual learners access to resources in their multiple languages
- Build on and integrate multilingual learners' languages, cultures, and traditions into their assessment experiences
- Use emerging technology and AI to support multilingual communication and learning responsibly

According to the *Oxford Review* (n.d.), "The primary difference between IQ (individual intelligence) and CQ or collective intelligence is the social dimension and the ability of groups to achieve unity of purpose, action and thought. Teams with high levels of CQ achieve a state of interdependence and flow when they are working together" (https://oxford-review.com/oxford-review-encyclopaedia-terms/collective-intelligence/).

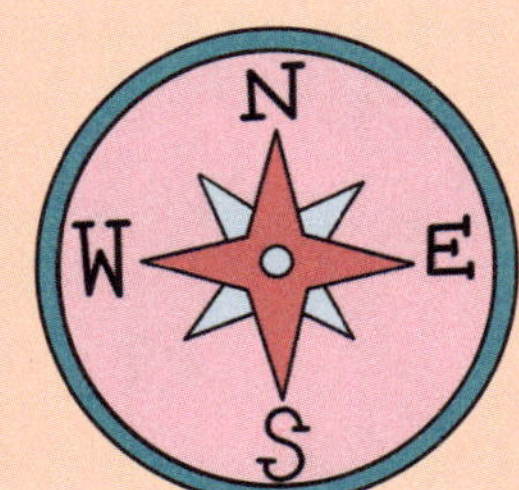

Driver 3: Establishing an equity-focused agenda that is achieved through collective effort

Why is this a key driver for collaborative assessment?

Historically marginalized students, especially multilingual learners, most likely have been negatively impacted by biased assessment practices and inequitable access to resources. Multilingual learners deserve accurate accounts of their language, literacy and academic growth and actionable and attainable goals for their chosen pathways to success.

How can we activate this driver?

- Learn about, with, and from your students and their families
- Insist on high expectations for all students
- Cocreate multiple ways for multilingual learners to demonstrate their learning
- Coconstruct learning experiences that build on student assets
- Advocate for fair, valid, and reliable assessment measures
- Collect evidence of student learning across content areas and over time
- Support student learning through multimodalities
- Become assessment literate

Driver 4: Supporting collaboration systematically among students, educators, and families

Why is this a key driver for collaborative assessment?

Schools, campuses, and districts serve multilingual learners better when there is coherence across the curricular, instructional, and assessment policies and practices. A systemic examination of and critical decision-making about evidence-based, research-informed best practices do not happen in boardrooms or behind closed doors. The challenge, urgency, and opportunity are to work together in a systematic way to create cohesion by establishing shared goals, clear protocols, and logistical support for collaborative assessment.

How can we activate this driver?

- Prioritize collaboration among all stakeholders
- Create structures and supports for collaborative learning environments and learning experiences
- Ensure or advocate for necessary resources
- Develop and act on an inclusive vision and mission for your school, campus, and district
- Assure both vertical and horizontal alignment of curriculum, instruction, and assessment across and within grades
- Advocate for inclusion and representation of each and every student
- Pledge to spotlight and nurture relationships among students, families, and educators

Start the Engine and Put the Gears in Place

We don't have to wait until teachers are hired for such a position to learn to collaborate! What if educators were better prepared for collaborative instruction and assessment during their preservice coursework? That is exactly what Molly A. Riddle, assistant professor of elementary mathematics education, and Kelli D. Bernedo, assistant professor of English as a new/second language, have initiated. Let's stay in Indiana and visit these teacher educators at Indiana University Southeast.

The Educator Preparation Program Co-Teaching with an Equity Lens (EPP CoTEL) framework that we created ensures that our teacher candidates are equipped with tools and systems to serve the diverse language needs of the P–12 students in their school communities. Our framework is designed to enhance content-specific college courses, so they address equity. We suggest professors seek out each other to engage in collaboration including:

- *Observing each other's classes, with an equity lens in mind*
- *Coplanning and coinstructing a specific unit of study related to equity*

- *Coassessing and coreflecting on each other's instructional practices*
- *Sharing resources in regard to multilingual learners' assets and needs*
- *Collaborating on research projects dedicated to equity*

These intentional, interdisciplinary collaborative opportunities allow teacher education professors in any discipline to expand their knowledge base and areas of expertise.

Let's visit Fort Wayne Community Schools in Indiana, where classroom teachers, ELD specialists, and coaches have recently engaged in a summer institute to explore collaborative practices. Figure 6.5 is one of many anchor charts that were cocreated to define what collaborative conversations about evidence of student learning look like and sound like.

Figure 6.5 Sticky Notes on Anchor Charts Indicating Agreement With Ideas

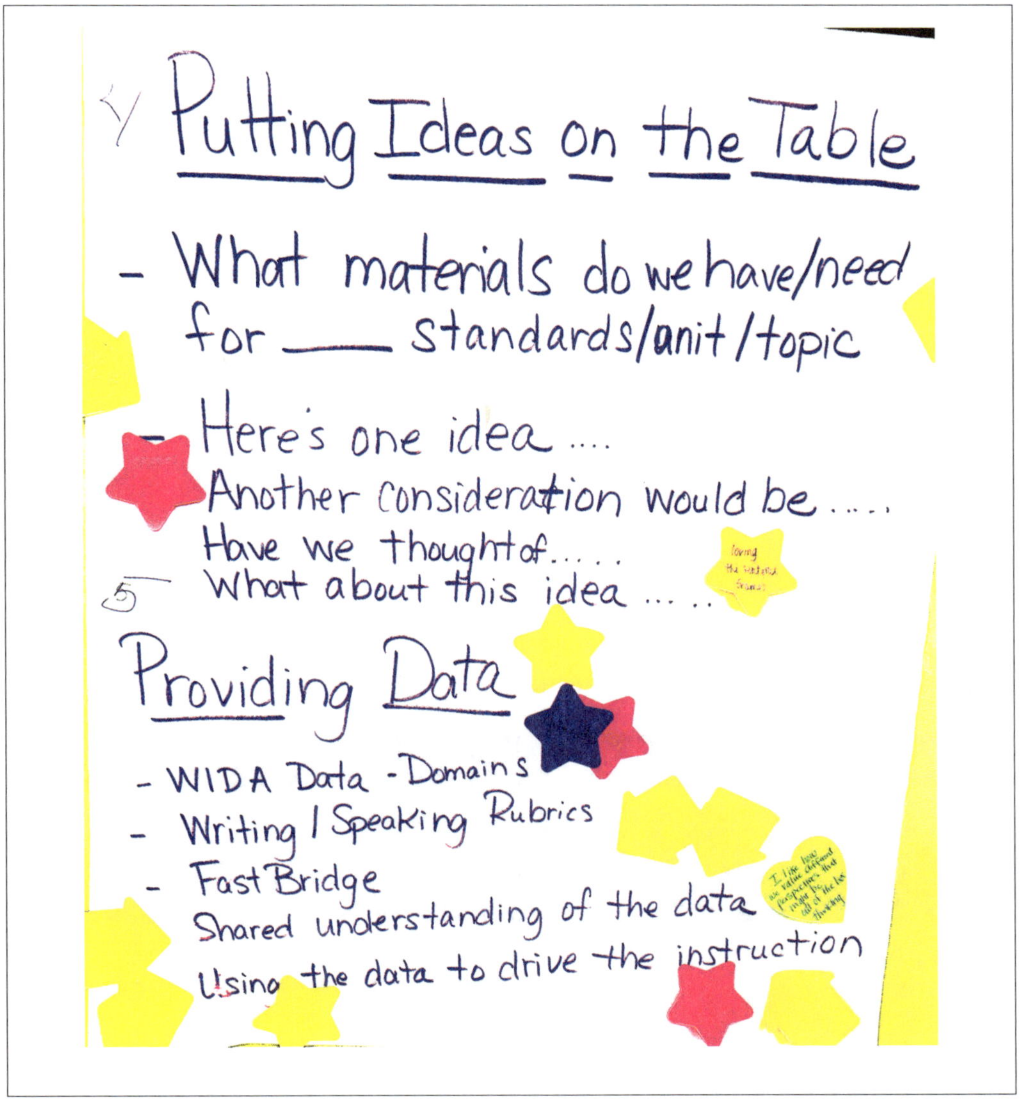

What Are Some Caveats/Challenges Along the Way?

Avoid a "My Way or the Highway" Approach!

Collaboration requires willing collaborators and more! Did you happen to know that the word collaborate comes from the Latin *collaborare* (in which *com/col* means "with, together, jointly" and *laborare*, being a cognate, means "labor or work") (https://www.merriam-webster.com/dictionary/collaborate)? So it implies that we have to work together on every level willingly and intentionally to forge partnerships and to jointly create something new. Did you also know that the word *assess* comes from the Latin *assessus* "a sitting by" (which is the past participle of *assidere/adsidere* "to sit beside")? In essence, assessment implies that the learner is integral to the process.

There may be many bumps along the way, some unexpected detours, and possibly delays. At times, we even have to turn around and get rerouted to avoid dead ends on our trip to collaboration. Some of the most frequently cited roadblocks to teacher collaboration include: (a) the limited amount of designated and protected collaboration time, often due to competing priorities, (b) the lack of equity and parity among stakeholders, (c) the absence of a shared understanding of students' assets and complex needs, and (d) the challenge to establish and sustain systemic leadership support.

What roadblocks, if any, have you identified in your context? How do they compare to the preceding four we listed? What have been some successful attempts to address these challenges?

To counteract these challenges, we are inviting you to focus on a key collaboration practice that might often be overlooked or taken for granted. In our field-based work, we have found that we cannot minimize the importance of partnership-building between and among all stakeholders. In Figure 6.6, we outline key partnership opportunities, emphasize ways to maximize the benefits of collaboration for each partnership, and make specific connections to collaborative assessment.

Figure 6.6 Maximizing Partnership Building for Collaborative Assessment

FORM COLLABORATIVE PARTNERSHIPS	MAXIMIZE COLLABORATIVE BENEFITS	APPLY THEM TO COLLABORATIVE ASSESSMENT
Students with students	Peers supporting each other	Engaging in peer assessment and providing feedback based on specified criteria
Students with teachers	Teachers acting as facilitators	Cocreating goals for learning, assessment tasks, and criteria of success

FORM COLLABORATIVE PARTNERSHIPS	MAXIMIZE COLLABORATIVE BENEFITS	APPLY THEM TO COLLABORATIVE ASSESSMENT
Teachers with teachers	Teachers combining their expertise and sharing their knowledge and experience	Looking at evidence of student learning from multiple angles; forming critical friends' groups to collaboratively assess, interpret, and report student work
Teachers with school leaders	Educators establishing and acting upon shared purposes and building a strong sense of community and collaborative culture	Establishing professional learning communities and cofacilitating data meetings that focus on student learning and systemic improvement of teaching
Leaders with leaders	Leaders learning together, creating systemic support for all stakeholders and enhancing an effective organizational model	Jointly reviewing data across grades, schools, and campuses; determining actionable next steps that represent and benefit the student body
Schools with colleges and universities	Institutions of higher education and K–12 schools pairing pre-service and in-service teacher education to field-based needs	Deepening professional learning around assessment for multilingual learners; engaging in action research and collaborative inquiry around assessment-related issues
Educators with families	Educators and families sharing responsibility for students through a climate of trust	Honoring and leveraging the cultural and linguistic assets of families across meaningful assessment practices

You might be thinking that collaboration within a school system is challenging enough, yet collaborating with diverse families may seem to be even more tenuous unless some conditions are in place. Debbie Zacarian, Margarita Calderón, and Margo Gottlieb (2021) suggest two requirements for all members of a school community for achieving a more inclusive, more collaborative instructional and assessment culture.

1. Challenge and move beyond commonly held traditional beliefs of family involvement that frequently appear to be a one-way street where typically teachers communicate with caregivers; schools invite parents to events. Consider actively shifting from parent involvement to reciprocal family engagement by creating the conditions for it to happen:
    a. Understanding and reflecting on cultural differences in how parents and caregivers define and enact their roles in their child's schooling and education
    b. Making all resources multilingual and disseminating information in multimodal ways
    c. Paying close attention to cross-cultural communication and potential misunderstandings
    d. Developing a shared commitment to multilingual language and literacy development

2. Appreciate parents or guardians as their child's first teachers.
   a. Family members play a crucial role as teachers, starting at birth.
   b. They also watch out, assess, monitor and celebrate their child's development, starting with counting all the tiny fingers and toes on the baby, observing developmental milestones, cheering on when the child faces new challenges, and applauding their achievements along the way.
   c. As members of the family unit, they instill languages, cultures, traditions, hopes, and dreams.
   d. Caregivers know their children in unique and wonderful ways that educators should recognize and build upon.

What Do We Need to Pack?

Not Too Much Extra Baggage!

Collaboration within a school, campus, or district, just like luggage, comes in different shapes and sizes. There is not one prescribed way to initiate a collaborative school culture nor one set of clear guidelines to maintain it; it depends on your destination and length of stay. As you continue to prepare for the next leg of your journey, take inventory of what choices you have and how to intentionally connect them to collaborative assessment. See Figure 6.7 for a summary of five types of instructional and non-instructional collaborations to engage in along with the goals and connections to assessment opportunities.

Figure 6.7 Collaborations Matched to Overarching Goals and Assessment Opportunities

COLLABORATIVE PRACTICES	GOALS	ASSESSMENT OPPORTUNITIES
1. Joint lesson and unit planning	• Establish attainable yet rigorous content-learning targets • Integrate content targets with language and literacy targets • Identify key learning experiences	• Carefully align goals and targets/ objectives to student learning • Design classroom assessment AS, FOR, and OF learning • Codesign assessment tools and measures • Coplan based on evidence for student learning over time • Prioritize daily assessment AS and FOR learning
2. Curriculum development, mapping, and alignment	• Plan out the scope and sequence for the course/year • Align language and literacy goals to core curricular goals	• Determine criteria for content attainment • Integrate language criteria • Establish prerequisites and codesign assessment tools • Cocreate products, performances, and projects representing assessment OF learning

COLLABORATIVE PRACTICES	GOALS	ASSESSMENT OPPORTUNITIES
3. Codeveloping instructional materials	• Insist on multimodal instructional materials • Select materials that provide access and support accelerated learning	• Use assessment data to design instructional materials • Build on evidence of student learning to enhance existing instructional resources • Prioritize assessment AS learning practices between students • Make provisions for resources in multiple languages
4. Coteaching	• Codeliver instruction through engagement in the entire collaborative instructional cycle • Use various models of instruction to establish equity between coteaching partners and students	• Engage in the complete instructional and assessment collaborative cycles • Use coteaching models that allow for collecting data and responding to students' needs based on evidence for student learning • Coassess by focusing on different foci of students' academic growth and language development • Interpret student data and make joint decisions based on students' characteristics, growth, and needs
5. Engaging in joint professional learning	• Support each others' planning, instructional, and assessment practices • Create a sustainable structure for improving day-to-day instruction and assessment	• Enhance your assessment literacy • Identify and enact changes to your teaching and assessment practices • Collaboratively study and review research related to instructional and assessment choices for multilingual learners • Deepen your knowledge and application of assessment • Engage in action research with colleagues • Create a balanced assessment system around AS, FOR, and OF learning approaches

In Chapter 2 we visited Jill Ayabei, in West Ada School District, Idaho, who shared her expertise and experiences with implementing the collaborative instructional cycle. This time, she offers insights into the importance of ongoing coaching support for collaborative assessment.

> *School building coaches can help to facilitate these conversations and ask good questions to lead to reflection and clear communication. If teachers are new to this type of collaboration, an instructional coach can guide these conversations, to validate views and feelings but also to challenge new ways of thinking. A coach can walk through data with teachers in non-evaluative ways to help them work together on how to improve specific areas of teaching and assessing. Observing peers in teaching and assessing can also help teachers to feel validated in what they are doing but to also challenge them in new ways.*

Which Pathways Should We Take?

Don't be Afraid of the Road Less Traveled!

Throughout the book, we have suggested multiple pathways to collaborative assessment for your multilingual learners in meaningful and actionable ways. We have presented alternative choices and guided you in your decision-making process through the collaborative instructional and assessment cycles. Let's revisit the three approaches to assessment—that is, assessment AS, FOR, and OF learning—by taking a closer look at the relationships that teachers and their multilingual learners build within a system of partnerships and a culture of collaboration:

- *Student-to-student interaction* gives multilingual learners the space and opportunity to become more self-directed and autonomous in their learning, to gauge their own progress, and to support their peers' learning.
- *Teacher-to-student interaction* allows both educators and multilingual learners to develop shared ownership of the instructional-assessment cycles, provide feedback and feedforward in support of student and teacher learning, and make shared decisions about next steps.
- *Teacher-to-teacher* interaction opens the door to sharing data, jointly analyzing and responding to evidence for student learning, and taking shared accountability for student growth.

See Figure 6.8 for a visual representation of three nested circles to remind us of the dynamic process of building trusting relationships for all assessment approaches.

Figure 6.8 A Collaborative System of Relationships Across Assessment AS, FOR, and OF Learning

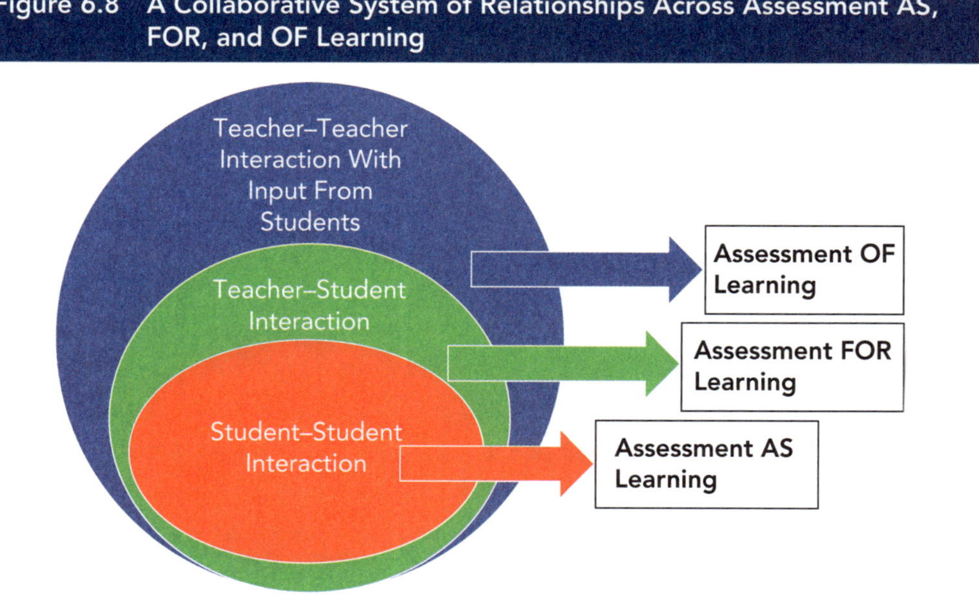

Moving From a Cycle to a Collaborative Assessment System

In Figure 2.10, we reviewed assessment AS, FOR, and OF learning with associated teacher actions and examples of tools. Here we examine the interaction between the three assessment approaches and the phases of the collaborative instruction cycle, indicating how multiple stakeholders participate and share in the process. Let's explore how collaboration permeates both instruction and assessment for greater transparency of meaningful information gleaned from the interaction between each assessment approach and instructional phase (See Figure 6.9).

Figure 6.9 Exploring the Intersection of the Approaches of Collaborative Assessment and the Phases of the Collaborative Instructional Cycle

	ASSESSMENT AS LEARNING . . . *STUDENTS . . .*	*ASSESSMENT FOR LEARNING . . .* STUDENTS AND TEACHERS WORK ON . . .	ASSESSMENT OF LEARNING . . . TEACHERS AND SCHOOL LEADERS INTERACT TO . . .
Coplanning	• Strategies for problem-solving with each other • Contributions to personal and group decision-making	• Setting goals for learning in one or more languages • Brainstorming projects of student interest	• Interpret score reports from high-stakes assessment • Contemplate grouping of students
Coinstructing	• Insights from academic conversations • Ideas, including multimodal representations of concepts	• Researching student-initiated projects • Providing feedback to one another	• Apply assessment results to initiate or strengthen schoolwide programs • Become assessment literate
Coassessing	• Academic, language, and social-emotional development goals • Evidence for approaching or meeting learning goals	• Crafting checklists and rubrics for performance tasks • Applying agreed-upon criteria for success to student samples	• Engage in professional learning regarding interpreting and applying results of state assessments • Share feedback on student and teacher learning
Coreflection	• Personal reflections on their language and literacy development • Joint reflections on their academic, language, and literacy achievements	• Establishing high expectations • Raising students' metacognitive, metalinguistic, and metacultural awareness	• Periodically review and evaluate short- and long-term goals • Review data for accountability purposes

Let's visit Bancroft Elementary, where collaboration is a key priority, according to Assistant Principal Christine Kennedy.

> *As part of the IB-PYP community, grade-level teams, which consist of classroom, ELD, special education, and intervention teachers, meet weekly to backward*

plan the units of inquiry. Teams utilize the IB action cycle to guide their collaborative process. This action cycle centers on three components:

Reflect: *How was learning impacted—as a whole class and by groups of students?*

Choose: *What will we do next, and what are the entry points for our learners?*

Act: How will we make learning happen? What will this look like in practice, and how will we embed multimodal approaches?

This year, as we focus on better supporting our multilingual learners, we have spent more time discussing how students can access instruction and demonstrate their understanding of learning alongside their language development. As teachers engage in collaborative planning, our instructional leaders support conversations by asking questions about how different approaches of assessments are being planned for (assessment AS, OF, and FOR learning) that embed multimodal opportunities (see Figure 6.10).

Figure 6.10 References for Assessment Approaches

ASSESSMENT APPROACHES	PURPOSE	EXAMPLES
Assessment FOR learning	An approach in which teachers, along with students, plan and use evidence from assessments and provide one another descriptive, criterion-referenced feedback to improve teaching and learning	• quizzes/tests • exit tickets • rubrics • performance tasks • graphic organizers • checklists • observations/anecdotal notes • running records • pre- & post-assessments • project-based learning • conferences • student self-reflection
Assessment AS learning	An approach in which students are agents of their own learning shown through self-reflection to show evidence against personal goals and criteria for success and communication of their learning to others	• student-created success criteria • peer reflection • student portfolios • presentations • learner profiles self-reflection • project-based learning • student-led conferences • exhibitions

ASSESSMENT APPROACHES	PURPOSE	EXAMPLES
Assessment OF learning	An approach in which teachers and students utilize assessment at the end of units to report on students' growth and achievement	• quizzes/tests • rubrics • observations/anecdotal notes • district & state standardized tests • district quarterly report cards

*Adapted from Margo Gottlieb (2021)

Teachers reflect on the various ways assessment can be utilized throughout their lessons and how they can better incorporate sensory, graphic, or interactive assessment practices to support content and language development. These conversations also help teachers consider how translanguaging is supported in their assessments. As teachers create their assessments, they create the success criteria of what they want their students to demonstrate (both with content understanding and language development) and create rubrics, checklists, and self-reflection tools.

Finally, to continue supporting the planning and implementation of multimodal assessments, we've created observation tools to reflect on during collaboration meetings, learning walks, and peer observations to see how students engage in learning. Utilizing these tools allows us to see which types of modalities teachers gravitate toward when planning for assessments and reflect on ways to adapt and adjust within upcoming units.

As coplanning, coinstructing, coassessing, and coreflecting intersect with assessment *AS*, *FOR*, and *OF* learning, what do you find are your areas of strengths and needs? What areas do you envision for professional learning throughout the school year?

What Should We Do Before Wrapping Up Our Trip?

Look Back to Where We Started!

In the introductory chapter, we established seven norms to ensure our journey is well-planned out, attainable, and meaningful. Do you recall some or perhaps all of them? Was there one that immediately resonated and stuck with you throughout your journey?

Here we revisit the seven norms through the lens of three stakeholder groups—students, families, and educators. Our intent is to look back at our assessment adventures and take in the vista from the top of the mountain, being mindful of some steps we took and choices we made:

1. ***When collaborative assessment is grounded in assets-based pedagogy***
    - *Students* are seen and heard; their gifts and talents are fully known, appreciated, and built upon
    - *Families* are valued for their assets and strengths, not for any perceived deficits
    - *Educators* intentionally look for what the students can do, where the students have been, and where they are headed in their learning discovery
2. ***When collaborative assessment is grounded in linguistically and culturally responsive and sustaining education***
    - *Students* interact with each other to coconstruct and respond to assessment tools that highlight what they know and can do; based on their languages, cultures, and experiences, they contribute to and understand their learning targets and goals
    - *Families and educators* develop trusting relationships and deep-rooted respect for each other by recognizing that student growth and achievement is to be shared
    - *Educators* unapologetically work on identifying, naming, and dismantling systemic inequities in assessment that typically hurt the most marginalized, most vulnerable populations, specifically, multilingual learners and multilingual learners with exceptionalities
3. ***When collaborative assessment is grounded in student voice and choice***
    - *Students* understand, take charge of, and articulate their learning needs and use multiple modalities and languages to show their knowledge and understanding
    - *Families* encourage their children to take pride in their identities, advocate for themselves, and share their experiences with peers without fear of bullying or dismissal
    - *Educators* abandon one-size-fits-all assessment practices that require one correct answer; instead, they aim to empower their students by giving them options in showing what they have learned and how to best demonstrate their new learning
4. ***When collaborative assessment is grounded in multilingualism***
    - *Students* may use all their linguistic resources available to express themselves
    - *Families* know that the languages and cultures of the home and community are to be honored and sustained

- *Educators* develop a critical stance on the bilingual/multilingual advantage, examine and overcome the implicit biases and stereotypes that often surround multilingualism, and celebrate their students' linguistic and cultural wealth

5. ***When collaborative assessment is grounded in learner variability***
   - *Students* feel valued for their unique strengths and preferences as learners and are encouraged to set challenging meaningful goals for themselves; they learn to take responsibility for their own learning and respond to timely feedback
   - *Families* feel affirmed that each child has strengths and based on those assets, will be held to the highest possible expectations
   - *Educators* recognize that every classroom consists of a group of heterogeneous learners; they accept their responsibility to create identity-safe learning environments and affirming, positive learning experiences that support all students to reach their full potential

6. ***When collaborative assessment is grounded in family engagement***
   - *Students'* funds of knowledge and identities, as well as cultural and out-of-school experiences, are integrated into assessment practices
   - *Families* engage in dialogic communication; they are not merely at the receiving end of information disseminated to them; they form partnerships with their children's teachers and other educators
   - *Educators* build open, meaningful relationships with families, and they share the responsibility for their students' academic, language, literacy, and social-emotional growth

7. ***When all assessment practices are grounded in a sustained culture of collaboration***
   - *Students* are agents of their own learning: Teaching and assessment are not things that simply happen to them, but they are cocreators of these experiences
   - *Families* understand that instruction and assessment are based on shared decision-making and it is their right to voice their opinions, make suggestions, and, at times, even overrule teacher or school recommendations
   - *Educators* intentionally create collaborative classroom and school communities where each member has a strong sense of belonging and where consistent and varied assessment practices based on principles of linguistic and cultural sustainability form a fair and equitable assessment system

It's time to take a moment and reflect on these seven norms in light of (a) what documented evidence you and your students have in support of the norms, (b) what areas to explore, and (c) what steps to take next (See Figure 6.11).

Figure 6.11 Reflecting on Norms for Collaborative Assessment Practices

NORMS FOR COLLABORATIVE ASSESSMENT PRACTICES	DOCUMENTED EVIDENCE IN SUPPORT OF THESE NORMS	AREAS TO EXPLORE	NEXT STEPS
1. Assets-based pedagogy			
2. Linguistically and culturally responsive and sustaining education			
3. Student voice and choice			
4. Multilingualism			
5. Learner variability			
6. Family engagement			
7. A culture of collaboration			

Where Do We Go Next?

Start New Collaborative Cycles . . . Just Don't Go Around in Circles!

Throughout our journey, we have introduced and elaborated the major pieces of a collaborative instructional and assessment system, anticipating that it would offer an organized structure for you and your colleagues to replicate. Starting with an overall vision of instructional and assessment cycles dedicated to multilingual learners and their educators, we have visited assessment AS, FOR, and OF learning as viable routes that complement each other to lead to a mutually agreed upon destination.

To ensure effective systemic implementation of collaborative instructional and assessment practices, we ask you and your team to take time to reflect. You are welcome to approach Figure 6.12 as a checklist (with yes/no responses) or a rating scale (from 1, not yet, to 4, fully), where you ask yourself or your team the following:

Figure 6.12 Evaluating Your Collaborative Instructional and Assessment System

___ Have you integrated the classroom assessment cycle into the instructional cycle to create an integrated whole?

___ Are there opportunities for sustained professional learning in collaboration and coassessment practices that incorporate culturally responsive and sustaining schooling for all teachers?

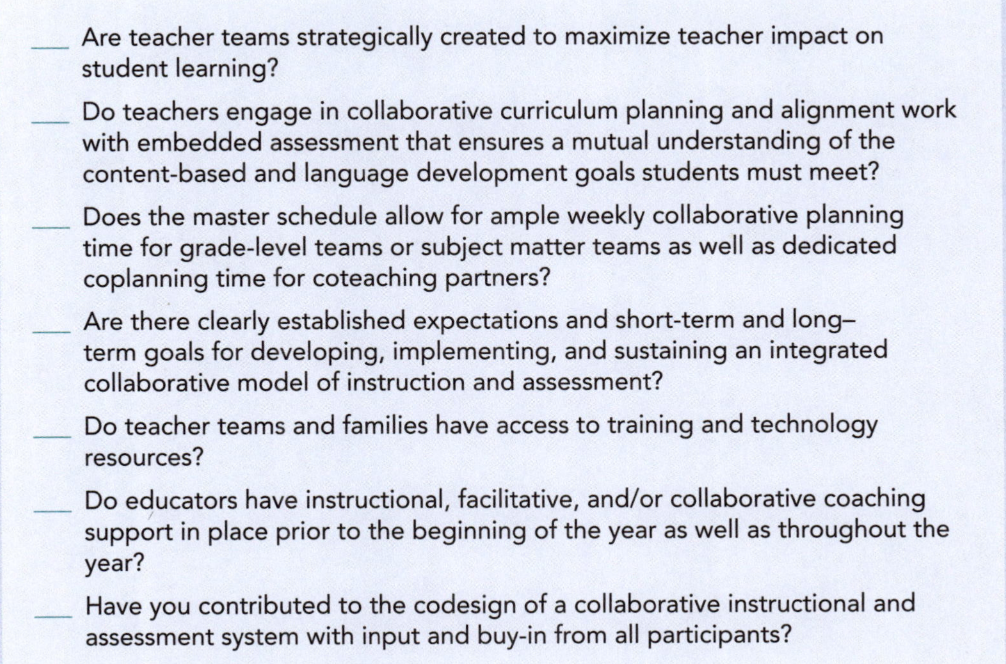

___ Are teacher teams strategically created to maximize teacher impact on student learning?

___ Do teachers engage in collaborative curriculum planning and alignment work with embedded assessment that ensures a mutual understanding of the content-based and language development goals students must meet?

___ Does the master schedule allow for ample weekly collaborative planning time for grade-level teams or subject matter teams as well as dedicated coplanning time for coteaching partners?

___ Are there clearly established expectations and short-term and long–term goals for developing, implementing, and sustaining an integrated collaborative model of instruction and assessment?

___ Do teacher teams and families have access to training and technology resources?

___ Do educators have instructional, facilitative, and/or collaborative coaching support in place prior to the beginning of the year as well as throughout the year?

___ Have you contributed to the codesign of a collaborative instructional and assessment system with input and buy-in from all participants?

In our travels, we have combined the collaborative model of assessment AS, FOR, and OF learning with the collaborative instructional cycle. We have illustrated how together the two cycles help create, foster, and grow relationships that support our teaching practices. We have shared values, beliefs, and promises for teaching and learning, and in doing so, we have attempted to break the isolation and insulation of teachers. By including students and teachers in a shared community of practice, we have forged lasting relationships and infused innovation along our trails. We hope that with collaborative assessment and instruction we bring intentionality to our profession, a positive influence on multilingual learners and their teachers, and a bright outlook ahead filled with enduring recollections of a memorable journey.

Postscript

The Katherine Johnson campus, highlighted in the vignettes woven throughout the book, is named after the famed mathematician, who overcame racial and gender barriers at her workplace. She was instrumental to the success of the NASA space program for over three decades. Among others, she worked with Mary Jackson and Dorothy Vaughan, a collaboration made famous in the book and movie *Hidden Figures*.

Katherine Johnson is known for lots of memorable sayings, this quote is a most fitting way to end our journey:

"We always worked as a team. It's never just one person."

Dorothy Vaughan

Katherine Johnson

Mary Jackson

Photo of American mathematician Dorothy Vaughan, "human computer" working at NACA, later NASA, from NASA Archive/Alamy. Portrait of Katherine Coleman Goble Johnson (born 1918) at NASA in 1966, from IanDagnall Computing/Alamy. Photo of Mary Jackson, American Mathematician and Aerospace Engineer from Science History Images/Alamy.

Glossary

Agency: student-centeredness in learning where students and teachers have the power of decision-making and effect classroom and school-level change.

Assessment AS learning: students' actively engage in the assessment process to further their own learning and autonomy, including student self- and peer reflection, setting personal goals, and interacting with peers and family members to (co)plan and communicate learning.

Assessment FOR learning: teachers and students coplan learning goals/targets and use corresponding evidence for learning to provide timely, descriptive, and actionable feedback for informing teaching and learning.

Assessment literacy: the concepts and qualities associated with designing, selecting, and using an array of measures along with examining data generated by them.

Assessment OF learning: teachers and school leaders coconstruct and reach consensus on criteria for success for learning and apply them (e.g., rubrics, descriptors) to students' products, projects, or performances; it also includes a range of standardized measures for achievement and language proficiency.

Classroom assessment: the collection, analysis, interpretation, and use of information during instructional routines to help inform instructional decisions.

Collaborative assessment: two or more students and/or educators working together and sharing the responsibility for planning, gathering, and interpreting data from some or all students in one or more classrooms.

Collaborative planning: two or more educators working together to plan instruction based on grade-appropriate standards and student data.

Common assessment: multiple classrooms using the identical measures, prompts, or projects along with the same interpretation tools for analyzing and using data in reliable ways.

Co-teaching: two or more educators jointly delivering instruction to one group of students in a shared learning space using a range of configurations.

Criteria for success: specific, measurable descriptors, often tied to learning goals and targets, that are shared by teachers and students.

Dialogic teaching: ongoing exchange and discussion between teachers and students or between students.

Feedback: concrete, constructive, and timely information that students give each other and their teachers or that teachers give students regarding progress toward meeting their learning goals or targets.

Formative assessment practices: providing contingent (spontaneous or planned) feedback to students during instruction.

Funds of identity: a set of resources shaped by lived experiences that are essential for self-definition, self-expression, and self-understanding.

Funds of knowledge: valuing the historical accumulation of knowledge along with linguistic and cultural capital of multilingual learners and their families and connecting those community resources to support learning in schools.

Gradual release of responsibility: supporting learners in moving toward independence and autonomy.

Inquiry-based learning: students assuming the practices and questioning of practitioners, such as journalists, mathematicians, or geologists, to coconstruct a knowledge base.

Integrated learning goals: combining content, language, multimodalities, and cultural referents in creating projects, performances, or products for units of learning.

Integrated learning targets: identifying student expected concepts or skills of a content area combined with their associated language and multimodalities for a lesson.

Interim or benchmark tests: the periodic administration of commercially available standardized measures to help educators determine the progress of students and predict the performance of students in annual high-stakes tests.

Makerspaces: students coconstructing and sharing their inventions or imaginative artifacts so that learners become creative producers rather than consumers.

Metacognitive awareness: consciously reflecting on and expressing your thinking process.

Metacultural awareness: consciously reflecting on your sociocultural identity and its shaping of how you learn and see the world.

Metalinguistic awareness: consciously reflecting on the nuances, comparisons, and uses of language within a single language or between two languages.

Multiliteracies: recognizing the hypergrowth of multilingual populations and the making of meaning that relies on technology and global digitalization to make sense of our multimodal world.

Multimodalities: combining written modes with oral, visual, audio, gestural, tactile, and spatial patterns of meaning to optimize understanding.

Peer assessment: classmates giving descriptive feedback on student work generally based on familiar criteria.

Place-based learning: immersing students in local heritage, cultures, landscapes, and experiences as a foundation for building and enacting a multidisciplinary curriculum.

Portfolio assessment: a systematic collection of original work samples that serves as evidence for a student's accomplishments and achievements, along with criteria for judging the work, in one or more content areas coupled with one of more languages.

Project-based learning: a series of related performance tasks around a theme and essential question that culminate in a product or performance for a unit of learning.

Reliability: uniformly interpreting student products from teacher to teacher or the consistency in applying results from assessment to make decisions.

Scaffolding: multimodal resources, including text coupled with sensory (e.g., photographs), graphic (e.g., T-charts), kinesthetic (e.g., movement), and linguistic (e.g., learning walls) supports embedded in instruction and assessment that assist multilingual learners across levels of language proficiency in constructing meaning from language and content.

Self-assessment: students' application of performance criteria or descriptors to monitor and interpret their own work to reflect on their language and content learning.

Socratic seminars: students engaging in formal discussion around open-ended questions sparking deep thinking along with articulating their own ideas and responding to others' thoughts.

Standardized testing: tests (historically with a multiple-choice format) that require students to answer the same question or questions in the same way to produce standard scores so that the performance of individuals or groups of students can be compared to one another or to specified criteria.

Street data: "qualitative, systematic, and experiential data that emerges at eye level (that) build on the tenets of culturally responsive education" (Safir & Dugan, 2021, p. 234).

Summative assessment practices: the "sum" of evidence for learning gathered at a point in time, such as at the culmination of units of learning or tests that are generally used for accountability purposes.

Tasks: two or more related instructional activities that generally involve multiple modalities or language domains (e.g., researching different sources, taking notes, and synthesizing the information) that fold into a project for a unit of learning (e.g., a multimedia presentation).

Tests: a systematic procedure for collecting samples of student performance at one point in time.

Translanguaging: the flexible and dynamic interaction between bilinguals where their full linguistic repertoires (multiple languages) are used to communicate in naturally occurring situations.

Validity: the extent to which the assessment matches its purpose and data are appropriate, complete, and linguistically and culturally responsive for the decisions made about students.

References

Arias, M. B. (2022). *Turning toward asset-based pedagogies for multilingual learners.* https://www.cal.org/wp-content/uploads/2022/10/Turning-Toward-Asset-Based-Pedagogies-1.pdf

Armstrong, M. (2024). From STEM to STEAM: Latino perspectives. *Language Magazine, 23*(5), 44.

Arnolds, J. (2022). Prioritising students in assessment for learning: A scoping review of research on students' classroom experience. *Review of Education, 10*(3), e3366. https://bera-journals.onlinelibrary.wiley.com/doi/epdf/10.1002/rev3.3366

August, D., & Shanahan, T. (Eds.), (2006). *Developing literacy in second-language learners: Report of the National Literacy Panel on Language-Minority Children and Youth.* https://eric.ed.gov/?id=ED556105

Auslander, L., & Yip, J. (2022). *School-wide systems for multilingual learner success: A roadmap for leaders.* Routledge.

Berger, R., Rugen, L., & Woodfin, L. (2014). *Leaders of their own learning: Transforming schools through student-engaged assessment.* Jossey-Bass.

Berryman, M., & Eley, E. (2019). Student belonging: Critical relationships and relationships. *International Journal of Inclusive Education, 23*(9), 985–1001.

Black, P., & Wiliam, D. (1998). Inside the black box: Raising standards through classroom assessment. *Phi Delta Kappan, 80*(2), 139–148.

Brookhart, S. M. (2023). *Classroom assessment essentials.* ASCD.

Brooks, J. S., Jean-Marie, G., Normore, A. H., & Hodgins, D. W. (2007). Distributed leadership for social justice: Exploring how influence and equity are stretched over an urban high school. *Journal of School Leadership, 17*(4), 378–408.

Bruno, J. (2021). *How to build student agency in your classroom.* NWEA. https://www.nwea.org/blog/2021/how-to-build-student-agency-in-your-classroom/

Callow, J. (2008). Show me: Principles for assessing students' visual literacy. *The Reading Teacher, 61*(8), 616–626.

CCNetwork. (2023, August). Impact area: Relationships. *R18CC & R19CC Newsletter.* https://earlylearning-network.unl.edu/wp-content/uploads/2023/04/ELN-Research-Brief_Relationships.pdf

Center for Leadership and Educational Equity. (n.d.). *Consultancy protocol.* https://schoolreforminitiative.org/doc/consultancy.pdf

Chandra, S., Chang, A., Day, L., Fazlullah, A., Liu, J., McBride, L., Mudalige, T., & Weiss, D. (2020). *Closing the K–12 digital divide in the age of distance learning.* Common Sense Media and Boston Consulting Group.

Choi, J., & Yi, Y. (2015). Teachers' integration of multimodality into classroom practices for English language learners. *TESOL Journal, 7*(2), 304–327.

Cohan, A., Honigsfeld, A., & Dove, M. G. (2020). *Team up, speak up, fire up! Teamwork to empower English learners.* ASCD.

Darling-Hammond, L., Flook, L., Cook-Harvey, C., Barron, B., & Osher, D. (2020). Implications for educational practice of the science of learning and development. *Applied Developmental Science, 24*(2), 97–140. https://doi.org/10.1080/10888691.2018.1537791

Davison, C., & Leung, C. (2012). Current issues in English language teacher-based assessment. *TESOL Quarterly, 43*(3), 393–415.

de Oliveira, L. C., & Westerlund, R. (Eds.). (2022). *Scaffolding for multilingual learners in elementary and secondary schools.* Routledge.

Dove, M. G., & Honigsfeld, A. (2018). *Co-teaching for English learners: A guide to collaborative planning, instruction, assessment, and reflection*. Corwin.

Dove, M. G., & Honigsfeld, A. (Eds.). (2020). *Co-teaching for English learners: Evidence-based practices and research-informed outcomes.* Information Age Publishing.

El Yaafouri, L. (2019). *6 tips for engaging the families of English language learners.* https://www.edutopia.org/article/6-tips-engaging-families-english-language-learners/

Esteban-Guitart, M., & Moll, L. C. (2014). Funds of identity: A new concept based on the funds of knowledge approach. *Culture and Psychology, 20*(1), 31–48.

Finley, T. (2014). Dipsticks: Efficient ways to check for understanding. *Edutopia.* https://www.edutopia.org/blog/dipsticks-to-check-for-understanding-todd-finley

Fisher, D., & Frey, N. (2023). *Visible learning and teaching multilingual learners: 5 considerations.* https://corwin-connect.com/2023/08/visible-learning-and-teaching-multilingual-learners-5-considerations/

Friend, M., & Cook, L. (2016). *Interactions: Collaboration skills for school professionals* (8th ed.). Pearson.

Fullan, M., & Quinn, J. (2024). *The drivers: Transforming learning for students, schools, and systems.* Sage.

Furze, L. (2023). *The A-I assessment scale.* https://leonfurze.com/2023/12/18/the-ai-assessment-scale-version-2/comment-page-1/

García, O., & Kleifgen, J. A. (2018). *Educating emergent bilinguals: Policies, programs, and practices for English learners.* Teachers College Press.

Gay, G. (2000). *Culturally responsive teaching: Theory, research, and practice.* Teachers College Press.

González, N., Moll, L., & Amanti, C. (2005). *Funds of knowledge: Theorizing practices in households, communities and classrooms.* Lawrence Erlbaum.

Gottlieb, M. (1995). Nurturing student learning through portfolios. *TESOL Journal, 5*(1), 12–14.

Gottlieb, M. (2003). *Large-scale assessment of English language learners: Addressing educational accountability in K–12 settings* (TESOL professional papers #6). Teachers of English to Speakers of Other Languages.

Gottlieb, M. (2006). *Assessing English language learners: Bridges from language proficiency to academic achievement.* Corwin.

Gottlieb, M. (2012). *Common language assessment for English learners.* Solution Tree.

Gottlieb, M. (2016). *Assessing English language learners: Bridges to equity connecting academic language proficiency to student achievement* (2nd ed.). Corwin.

Gottlieb, M. (2021). *Classroom assessment in multiple languages: A handbook for teachers.* Corwin.

Gottlieb, M. (2022a). *Assessment in multiple languages: A handbook for school and district leaders.* Corwin.

Gottlieb, M. (2022b). *How can multilingual learners and their teachers make a difference in classroom assessment?* Center for Applied Linguistics.

Gottlieb, M. (2023a). From monolingual assessment to assessment in multiple languages. In I. Soto, S. Snyder, M. E. Calderón, M. Gottlieb, A. Honigsfeld, J. Lachance, M. Marshall, D. Nungaray, R. Flores, & L. Scott (Eds.), *Breaking down the monolingual wall: Essential shifts for multilingual learners' success* (pp. 91–120). Corwin.

Gottlieb, M. (2023b). *Right from the start: Enriching learning experiences for multilingual learners through multiliteracies.* Center for Applied Linguistics.

Gottlieb, M. (2024). *Assessing multilingual learners: Bridges to empowerment* (3rd ed.). Corwin.

Gottlieb, M., & Calderón, M. (2024). *Together we can! ¡Juntos podemos!* Velasquez Press.

Gottlieb, M., & Ernst-Slavit, G. (2019). Promoting educational equity in assessment practices. In L. C. de Oliveira (Ed.), *The handbook of TESOL in K–12* (pp. 129–148). John Wiley & Sons.

Gottlieb, M., & Honigsfeld, A. (2020). From assessment *of* learning to assessment *for* and *as* learning. In M. E. Calderón, M. G. Dove, D. S. Fenner, M. Gottlieb, A. Honigsfeld, T. W. Singer, S. Slakk, I. Soto, & D. Zacarian. *Breaking down the wall: Essential shifts for English learners' success* (pp. 135–160). Corwin.

Gottlieb, M., & Katz, A. (2020). Assessment in the classroom. In C. Chappelle (Ed.), *The concise encyclopedia of applied linguistics* (pp. 44–51). John Wiley & Sons.

Hammond, Z. (2015). *Culturally responsive teaching & the brain: Promoting authentic engagement and rigor among culturally and linguistically diverse students.* Corwin.

Harapnuik, D. (2020). *Assessment OF/FOR/AS learning.* https://www.harapnuik.org/?p=8475

Hattie, J., & Timperley, H. (2007). The power of feedback. *Review of Educational Research, 77*(1), 81–112.

Heritage, M. (2016). Assessment for learning: Co-regulation *in* and *as* student–teacher interaction. In D. Laveault & L. Allai (Eds.), *Assessment for learning: Meeting the challenge of implementation. The enabling power of assessment* (Vol. 4, pp. 327–343). Springer.

Heritage, M. (2022). *Formative assessment: Making it happen in the classroom* (2nd ed.). Corwin.

Hilliard, J. F., & Gottlieb, M. (2021, June). Seeing multilingual learners' reflections en EL ESPEJO. *Bilingual basics, the newsletter of the bilingual multilingual education interest section, TESOL international association.*

Hilliard, J. F., & Gottlieb, M. (2023). *The ESPEJO curriculum framework: Abbreviated version.* The ESPEJO Curriculum Framework for the Acero Charter School Network.

Hira, A., & Hynes, M. (2018, June 3). People, means, and activities: A conceptual framework for realizing the educational potential of makerspaces. *Education Research International, 2018*, 1–10, Article ID 6923617. https://doi.org/10.1155/2018/6923617

Honigsfeld, A., & Dove, M. G. (2019). *Collaborating for English learners: A foundational guide to integrated practices.* Corwin.

Honigsfeld, A., & Dove, M. G. (Eds.). (2021). *Portraits of collaboration: Educators working together to support multilingual learners.* Seidlitz.

Honigsfeld, A., & Dove, M. G. (2022). *Co-planning: Five essential practices to integrate curriculum and instruction for English learners.* Corwin.

IES REL Pacific. (2024). *Including voice in education: Addressing equity through student and family voice in classroom learning.* https://ies.ed.gov/ncee/edlabs/infographics/pdf/REL_PA_Including_Voice_in_Education_Addressing_Equity_Through_Student_and_Family_Voice_in_Classroom_Learning.pdf

Ishimaru, A. M., Torres, E. K., Salvador, J. E., Lott, J., Cameron Williams, D. M., & Tran, C. (2016). Reinforcing deficit, journeying toward equity: Cultural brokering in family engagement initiatives. *American Educational Research Journal, 53*, 850–882.

Jacobs, G. E. (2013). *Designing assessments: A multiliteracies approach.* http://multiliterateteachers.pbworks.com/w/file/fetch/79941050/Designing%20Assessments%20A%20Multiliteracies%20Approach.pdf

James, M. J. (2023). Assessing and learning, and learning to learn. In R. J. Tierney, F. Rizvi, & K. Ercikan (Eds.), *International encyclopedia of education* (4th ed., pp. 10–20). Elsevier.

Jenkins, M. C., & Murawski, W. W. (2024). *Connecting high-leverage practices to student success.* Corwin.

Jeynes, W. (2012). A meta-analysis of the efficacy of different types of parental involvement programs for urban students. *Urban Education, 47*(4), 706–742.

Jung, L. A. (2023). *Seen, heard, and valued: Universal design for learning and beyond.* Corwin.

Kalantzis, M., Cope, B., & Harvey, A. (2003). Assessing multiliteracies and the new basics. *Assessment in Education: Principles, Policy & Practice, 10*(1), 15–26.

Kang, H., Thompson, J., & Windschitl, M. (2014). Creating opportunities for students to show what they know: The role of scaffolding in assessment tasks. *Science Education, 98*(4), 674–704. https://escholarship.org/content/qt1q97v3bz/qt1q97v3bz.pdf?t=nm2len

Kim, J., Lee, H., & Cho, Y. H. (2022). Learning design to support student AI collaboration: Perspectives of leading teachers for AI in education. *Education and Information Technologies, 27*, 6069–6104.

Ladson-Billings, G. (1995). Toward a theory of culturally relevant pedagogy. *American Educational Research Journal, 32*(3), 465–491.

Lin, L. (2015). *Investigating Chinese HE EFL classrooms: Using collaborative learning to enhance learning.* Springer-Verlag Berlin Heidelberg.

Listenwise. (2022). *Multimodal learning as an effective scaffold.* https://listenwise.com/wp-content/uploads/2022/12/Multimodal-Learning_Listenwise-Whitepaper2022.pdf

May, S. (Ed.). (2014). *The multilingual turn: Implications for SLA, TESOL, and bilingual education.* Routledge.

Malone, M. E. (2013). The essentials of assessment literacy: Contrasts between testers and users. *Language Testing, 30*(3), 329–344.

Mercer, N. (2003). The educational value of "dialogic talk" in "whole-class dialog." In Qualifications and Curriculum Authority (Ed.), *New perspectives on spoken English in the classroom: Discussion papers* (pp. 73–76). Qualifications and Curriculum Authority.

Michigan Assessment Consortium. (2017). *Assessment literacy standards.* https://www.michigan.gov/mde/services/student-assessment/assessment-literacy

Miller, C. F., Kochel, K. P., Wheller, L. A., Updegraff, K. A., Fobes, R. A., Martin, C. L., & Honish, L. D. (2017). The efficacy of a relationship intervention in 5th grade. *Journal of School Psychology, 61*, 75–88.

Mohan, B. (1986). *Language and content.* Addison-Wesley.

Morita-Mullaney, P. (2022, May 24). *Advocating for multilingual learners: Educators at the nexus of creativity and resistance.* MATSOL, Virtual Keynote presentation.

Murawski, W. W., & Lochner, W. W. (2017). *Beyond co-teaching basics: A data-driven, no-fail model for continuous improvement.* ASCD.

National Academies of Sciences, Engineering, and Medicine (NASEM). (2017). *Promoting the educational successes of children and youth learning English: Promising futures.* The National Academies Press. https://nap.nationalacademies.org/read/24677/chapter/2

National Academy of Education. (2020). *Reaping the rewards of the reading for understanding initiative.* Author.

National Committee for Effective Literacy (NCEL). (2022). *Toward comprehensive effective literacy policy and instruction for English learner/emergent bilinguals students.* https://multilingualliteracy.org/wp-content/uploads/2022/04/21018-NCEL-Effective-Literacy-White-Paper-FINAL_v2.0.pdf

National Research Council. (2000). *How people learn: Brain, mind, experience, and school* (expanded edition). The National Academies Press. https://nap.nationalacademies.org/read/9853

New York State Education Department (NYSED). (2019). *Culturally responsive-sustaining education framework.* https://www.nysed.gov/sites/default/files/programs/crs/culturally-responsive-sustaining-education-framework.pdf

Nordmeyer, J., & Honigsfeld, A. (2023, November). Building capacity FOR collaboration and THROUGH collaboration. *Language Magazine, 24*, 19–23.

North Carolina Department of Public Instruction. (2024). *North Carolina generative AI implementation recommendations and considerations for PK–13 public schools.* https://go.ncdpi.gov/AI_Guidelines

O'Connell, M. J., & Vandas, K. (2015). *Partnering with students: Building ownership of learning.* Corwin.

OECD. (2019). OECD future of education and skills, 2030. Conceptual learning framework. *Student Agency for 2030.* https://www.oecd.org/education/2030-project/teaching-and-learning/learning/student-agency/Student_Agency_for_2030_concept_note.pdf

Otheguy, R., García, O., & Reid, W. (2015). Clarifying translanguaging and deconstructing named languages: A perspective from linguistics. *Applied Linguistics Review, 6*(3), 281–307. https://www.degruyter.com/document/doi/10.1515/applirev-2015-0014/html

Oxford Review. (n.d.). *Collective intelligence.* https://oxford-review.com/oxford-review-encyclopaedia-terms/collective-intelligence/

Paris, D. (2012). Culturally sustaining pedagogy: A needed change in stance, terminology, and practice. *Educational Researcher, 41*(3), 93–97.

Pearson, P. D., McVee, M. B., & Shanahan, L. E. (2019). In the beginning: The historical and conceptual genesis of the gradual release of responsibility. In M. B. McVee, E. Ortlieb, J. S. Reichenberg, & P. D. Pearson (Eds.), *The gradual release of responsibility in literacy research and practice. Literacy, research, practice, and evaluation* (Vol. 10, pp. 1–21). Emerald Publishing Limited.

Popham, W. J. (2011). *Transformative assessment in action: An inside look into applying the process.* ASCD.

Popham, W. J. (2019). *Classroom assessment: What teachers need to know.* Pearson.

Proctor, C. P., Silverman, R. D., & Jones, R. L. (2021). Centering language and student voice in multilingual literacy instruction. *The Reading Teacher, 75*(3), 255–267.

Promise of Place. (n.d.). *What is place-based education?* https://promiseofplace.org

Rajendram, S. (2019). *Translanguaging as an agentive, collaborative and socioculturally responsive pedagogy for multilingual learners* [Doctoral dissertation, University of Toronto]. https://tspace.library.utoronto.ca/handle/1807/97590

Rothstein, D., & Santana, L. (2011). *Make just one change: Teach students to ask their own questions.* Harvard Education Press.

Sackstein, S. (2024). *Beyond a highlight reel: Portfolios as dynamic workspaces.* ASCD.

Safir, S., & Dugan, J. (2021). *Street data: A next-generation model for equity, pedagogy, and school transformation.* Corwin.

Sanders-Smith, S. C., & Dávila, L. T. (2021). "It has to be in a natural way": A critical exploration of co-teaching relationships in trilingual preschool classrooms in Hong Kong. *Journal of Multilingual and Multicultural Development, 45*(4), 1182–1196. https://www.tandfonline.com/doi/full/10.1080/01434632.2021.1957902

Schellekens, L. H., Bok, H. G. J., de Jong, L. H., van der Schaaf, M. F., Kremer, W. D. J., & van der Vleuten, C. P. M. (2021). A scoping review on the notions of Assessment as Learning (AaL), Assessment for Learning (AfL), and Assessment of Learning (AoL). *Studies in Educational Evaluation, 71,* 101094. https://doi.org/10.1016/j.stueduc.2021.101094

Schissel, J., Leung, C., López-Gopar, M., & Davis, J. R. (2018). Multilingual learners in language assessment: Assessment design for linguistically diverse communities. *Language and Education, 12*(2), 167–182.

Shepard, L. A. (2021). *Ambitious teaching and equitable assessment: A vision for prioritizing learning, not testing.* https://www.aft.org/ae/fall2021/shepard

Sherin, M. G., Jacobs, V. R., & Philipp, R. A. (Eds.). (2011). *Mathematics teacher noticing: Seeing through teachers' eyes.* Routledge.

Sherris, A. (2008). Integrated content and language instruction. *CAL digest.* Center for Applied Linguistics.

Snow, M. A., Met, M., & Genesee, F. (1989). A conceptual framework for the integration of language and content in second/foreign language instruction. *TESOL Quarterly, 23*(2), 201–217.

Soto, I., Snyder, S., Calderón, M. E., Gottlieb, M., Honigsfeld, A., Lachance, J., Marshall, M., Nungaray, D., Flores, R., & Scott, L. (2024). *Breaking down the monolingual wall.* Corwin.

Swaffield, S. (2011). Getting to the heart of authentic assessment for learning. *Assessment in Education: Principles, Policy, & Practice, 18*(4), 433–444.

Swain, M. (2006). Languaging, agency and collaboration in advanced second language proficiency. In H. Byrnes (Ed.), *Advanced language learning: The contributions of Halliday and Vygotsky* (pp. 95–108). Continuum.

TESOL International Association. (2024). *The 6 principles for exemplary teaching of English learners* (2nd ed.). TESOL Press.

The New London Group. (1996). A pedagogy of multiliteracies: Designing social futures. *Harvard Educational Review, 66*(1), 60–93.

U.S. Department of Education. (2023). *Biden-Harris administration launches "Being bilingual is a superpower" to promote multilingual education for a diverse workforce.* https://www.ed.gov/news/press-releases/biden-harris-administration-launches-%E2%80%9C-being-bilingual-superpower%E2%80%9D-promote-multilingual-education- diverse-workforce

U.S. Department of Education, OELA. (2023). *Newcomer toolkit.* https://ncela.ed.gov/sites/default/files/2023-06/NewcomerToolkit-06222023-508_OELA.pdf

U.S. Department of Education, Office of Educational Technology. (2017). *Reimagining the role of technology in education: 2017 national education technology plan update.* https://tech.ed.gov/files/2017/01/NETP17.pdf

U.S. Department of Education, Office of Educational Technology. (2023). *K–12 digital infrastructure brief: Adequate and future proof.* https://tech.ed.gov/files/2023/08/FINAL_Adequate_FutureProof.pdf

U.S. Department of Education, Office of Educational Technology. (2024a). *A call to action for closing the digital access, design, and use divides: 2024 national educational technology plan.* https://tech.ed.gov/files/2024/01/NETP24.pdf

U.S. Department of Education, Office of Educational Technology. (2024b). *Priorities.* https://tech.ed.gov/priorities/

van Es, E. (2021). *Teacher noticing: What is it and why does it matter for teaching?* UCI Teacher Academy. https://teacheracademy.uci.edu/teacher-noticing-what-is-it-and-why-does-it-matter-for-teaching/

Vatterott, C. (2024). *Student mental health: What's autonomy got to do with it?* (Vol. 81, No. 5). ASCD.

Villa, R. A., Thousand, J. S., & Nevin, A. I. (2013). *A guide to co-teaching: New lessons and strategies to facilitate student learning* (3rd ed.). Corwin.

Vygotsky, L. S. (1978). *Mind in society: The development of higher psychological processes.* Harvard University Press.

Walqui, A., & van Lier, L. (2010). *Scaffolding the academic success of adolescent English language learners: A pedagogy of promise.* WestEd.

WIDA. (2019). *The WIDA can do philosophy.* The Board of Regents of the University of Wisconsin System. https://wida.wisc.edu/sites/default/files/resource/WIDA-CanDo-Philosophy.pdf

WIDA. (2020). *WIDA English language development standards framework, 2020 edition: Kindergarten-grade 12.* Board of Regents of the University of Wisconsin System.

WIDA. (2023). *Marco de los estándares del desarrollo auténtico del lenguaje español de WIDA Kinder al 12 grado.* Board of Regents of the University of Wisconsin System.

Wiggins, G., & McTighe, J. (2005). *Understanding by design* (2nd ed.). ASCD.

Wiggins, G., & McTighe, J. (2011). *The understanding by design guide to creating high-quality units.* Association for Supervision and Curriculum Development.

Wiliam, D. (2011). *Embedded formative assessment.* Solution Tree.

Wolpert-Gawron, H. (2016). What the heck is inquiry-based learning? *Edutopia.* https://www.edutopia.org/blog/what-heck-inquiry-based-learning-heather-wolpert-gawron

Yin, S., Chen, F., & Chang, H. (2022). Assessment as learning: How does peer assessment function in students' learning? *Frontiers in Psychology, 13,* 912568. https://www.ncbi.nlm.nih.gov/pmc/articles/PMC9271947/

Yoon, B. (2022). *Effective teacher collaboration for English language learners: Cross-curricular insights from K–12 settings.* Routledge.

Zacarian, D., Calderón, M., & Gottlieb, M. (2021). *Beyond crisis: Overcoming linguistic and cultural inequities in communities, schools, and classrooms.* Corwin.

Zwiers, J. (2019). *Academic conversations: Ideas for improving learning through classroom talk.* Stenhouse.

Index

CORWIN
A Sage Company